**SILENCE
IN THE FICTION
OF
ELIE WIESEL**

BY

MONA BERMAN

Illustrations by Kim Berman from the series of dry points "After Rembrandt ... an interpretation of silence."

Copyright © 2001 Mona Berman

All rights reserved.

Produced by comPress   www.compress.co.za

CONTENTS

PREFACE — v

INTRODUCTION — 1
Wiesel and The Literature of Testimony

CHAPTER 1 — 17
Critical responses to Wiesel's writings and an evaluation of his narrative strategies

CHAPTER 2 — 35
Scenic silence in *Night, Dawn* and *The Accident*

CHAPTER 3 — 59
The silence through the dialogues in *The Town Beyond the Wall*

CHAPTER 4 — 79
Silence as a narrative presence in *The Gates of the Forest*

CHAPTER 5 — 101
The silence between the tales in *A Beggar in Jerusalem*

CHAPTER 6 — 121
The silence of the narrators in *The Oath*

CHAPTER 7 — 143
Conclusion: The mute narrator in *The Testament*

APPENDIX: INTERVIEW — 165
NOTES — 179
WORKS BY WIESEL — 183
BIBLIOGRAPHY — 185
ABOUT THE AUTHOR — 186

PREFACE

I dedicate this book to the memory of my mother and my father. It was from them that I learned that to be a Jew is not only my birthright, but a choice I could make with joy and gratitude. From an early age I was haunted by the Holocaust experience, not because it affected my life personally, but because of its total incomprehensibility. I began reading the literature of survivors, historians, philosophers, poets and novelists. Instead of understanding more, I understood less. I even believed that the research undertaken for this project on Elie Wiesel would provide some answers to my quest. Yet I discovered that there are no answers, there are only questions.

One of the memorable reading experiences of my life was in 1969 on board a ship from France to the United States when by chance I discovered in the ship's library Wiesel's *The Gates of the Forest*. I read it, and having completed it, I immediately reread it. I had the feeling then of not having grasped its full significance, of having missed out areas in the text and of having to interpret the pauses, gaps, fragments and the discontinuity in the story. Wiesel then was a relatively unknown writer, and I did not have the key to the gates he had opened for me. Only much later, after having traced his previous writings and by filling my bookshelf and my memory with his books that emerged every few years, did I come to the realisation that Wiesel is one of the few writers I am acquainted with who uses silence in his fiction as a narrative device.

Wiesel was born in 1928 in a small Hungarian town, Sighet, "somewhere in the Carpathian mountains". His life and work have been well documented by Molly Abromowitz in her book *Elie Wiesel: A Bibliography*. His father, Shlomo, a middle-class shopkeeper instilled values of Western humanism in his son, while his mother Sarah, insisted that the young boy received a Torah education, which included the study of the Talmud, the mystical doctrines of the Kabbalah and the teachings of the Hasidic masters. In the spring of 1944 the Jews of Transylvania were rounded up on orders of the Germans. Wiesel, his parents and three sisters were deported on a cattle train to Auschwitz concentration camp in Poland. His father was killed by the Nazis in his presence, and his mother and younger sister died at Auschwitz. In 1945 he was sent to Buchenwald concentration camp as a slave labourer. After the American Liberation, Wiesel wanted to go to Palestine, but this was prevented by British immigration restrictions. He, together with 400 other orphans, boarded a train headed for Belgium. The train was diverted to France where the passengers were asked whether they wished to become French citizens. Wiesel, unable to understand French, failed to respond and became stateless. Settling in Normandy, he soon mastered French and later moved to Paris, where from 1948 to 1951 he studied philosophy at the Sorbonne, earning his living as a choir director and as a teacher of the Bible. He spent some time in India, where he studied comparative asceticism and acquired a knowledge of English. In 1948, he was sent by a French newspaper to report on the Israeli independence struggle and became the chief foreign correspondent for the Tel Aviv daily, Yediot Achronot. In 1956, while reporting on the United Nations for the newspaper, he was struck by a taxicab in Time Square. While recovering in a New York City hospital, he was persuaded to apply for United States citizenship, which he finally obtained in 1963.

Wiesel has been appointed Chairman of the U.S. Holocaust Memorial Council and is Andrew Mellon

Professor in the Humanities at Boston University. Among the many literary honours bestowed on him are France's Prix Rivarol, Prix Medicis and the Prix Inter 1980, the Jewish Heritage Award and the National Jewish Book Council Award.

Shortly after completing my thesis 'Elie Wiesel's Fictional Universe: The Paradox of the Mute Narrator' in fulfilment of the requirements for the degree of Master Arts in the department of English at Rhodes University, Grahamstown, in November 1985, Elie Wiesel was awarded the Nobel Peace Prize. He dedicated it to his fellow survivors who "have tried to do something with their memory, with their silence, with their life ... they have given an example to humankind not to succumb to despair." With the prize money he established 'The Elie Wiesel Foundation' to advance the cause of human rights and peace throughout the world by organising conferences and symposiums to bring out awareness of injustices and hate.

Few Nobel prize winners have achieved as much acclaim, worked as tirelessly and inspired so many people throughout the world with their moral vision. He has continued to pursue a distinguished scholastic career, teaching classes at Boston University, as well as lecturing extensively at universities throughout the world. He still finds time to write Hasidic, Talmudic and Biblical Tales, as well as fictional works. To date, he has written 36 books.

I would like to acknowledge and thank those people who believed in the validity of my research over many years and who now have encouraged and supported me to have my work published as a book for general readership. It is my fervent hope that the passion I feel for Elie Wiesel's writing as testimony will be shared by people who will be enriched not only by the stories he tells but by the way he tells them.

INTRODUCTION:
WIESEL AND THE LITERATURE OF TESTIMONY

The prevalent attitude of literary critics towards the works of Elie Wiesel is exemplified by David Daiches's contention, in a review in *Commentary*, that Holocaust literature is impossible to discuss "in the terms which one would normally employ in reviewing fiction". He believes that it should be viewed as important documentary evidence "dealing with something which must perpetually haunt everyone old enough to have lived through World War 2. It is my contention that literary analysis can and should be applied to Wiesel's fiction.

In attempting to assess the literature of the Holocaust, critics and scholars have been tempted to assign causes to the event, to perceive it in terms of historical perspectives and according to social and psychological antecedents. Causation, in this sense, implies that it is possible for any society, given the right conditions, to produce such a barbarity. However, as Lacey Baldwin Smith says in his Foreword to *Dimensions of the Holocaust*, "The only explanation of a genuinely unique event is no explanation at all". This proposition, supported by J. L. Talmon's lecture at a symposium "Holocaust and Rebirth", provides a viewpoint which I believe is significant for a background to this study:

> Never since the dawn of history had the world witnessed such a campaign of extermination. This was not an explosion of religious fanaticism; not a wave of pogroms, the work of incited mobs running amok or led by a ringleader; not the riots of soldiery gone wild or drunk with victory and wine; not the fear-wrought psychosis of revolution or civil war that rises and subsides like a whirlwind. It was none of these. An entire nation was handed over by a 'legitimate' government to murderers organised by the authorities and trained to hunt and kill, with one single provision, that everyone, the entire nation be murdered – men and women, old and young, healthy and sick and paralysed, everyone without any chance of even one of those condemned to extermination escaping his fate.
>
> After they had suffered hunger, torture, degradation and the humiliation inflicted on them by their tormentors to break them down, to rob them of the last shred of human dignity, and to deprive them of any strength to resist and perhaps any desire to live, the victims were seized by the agencies of the state and brought from the four corners of Hitlerite Europe to the death camps, to be killed, individually or in groups, by the murderer's

> bullets over graves dug by the victims themselves, or in the slaughterhouses constructed especially for human beings. For all the condemned there was no judge to whom to appeal for a redress of injustice; no government from which to ask protection and punishment for the murderers; no neighbour on whose gate to knock and ask for shelter; and no God to whom to pray for mercy. (11-12)

In its conscious and explicit planning, in its systematic execution, in the absence of any emotion in the remorselessly applied decision to exterminate all Jews, the Holocaust differed from killings, massacres and bloodshed perpetrated throughout history. Because of its magnitude and ontological nature, the event remains central and unique in history. As a result of the Holocaust, man's relationship to his creator, to society, to politics, to literature, to his fellow man and to a himself had to be re-examined.

After Auschwitz, language was corrupted to a point where words had lost their meaning. There was a point beyond which language could be translated into experience. The whole story could not be told because there was no adequate means by which to tell it. All a writer could do was to communicate the impossibility of communication: he had to tell less than more, to write not with words but against words. The result was that survivors wrote about the pre-Holocaust period of their past, about the *shtetls*, the little villages of Eastern Europe. They wrote memoirs to bring back to life people and places that had been destroyed and consumed in fire. Those who had lived through the event could never entirely reveal it because the words linking them to their experience were ineffectual and unfamiliar. They could neither identify with the situation because of its unique nature, nor could they identify with the victims and executioners, both of whom were representatives of organised society. As Wiesel explains in *Dimensions of the Holocaust*:

> For the factories of death to emerge and function, philosophers and psychologists, scholars and engineers, attorneys and aristocrats, lovers of art and poetry, criminals and sadists had to join forces. (6)

Similarly, all categories were included among the victims. All Jews in Europe shared the same fate. The event robbed man of all his masks, his values, his aspirations and his comprehension. The basis for confidence in reality was destroyed; the experience had no precedent. Language in this context became impotent.

In *Language and Silence*, George Steiner examines T.W. Adorno's proposition that "to write poetry after Auschwitz is barbaric". Steiner is one of the first critics to provide a searching analysis of the tensions confronting the writer faced with the inadequacy of language to describe the reality of the Holocaust. He argues that the only effective way the writer can deal with the possibility of the ineffable is through silence: "The world of Auschwitz lies outside speech as it lies outside reason". Many of Steiner's ideas about the relationship between language and silence are derived from the notion that under Nazism "words were committed to saying things no human mouth should every have said and no paper made by man should ever have been inscribed with". Yet, a great deal of literature has emerged from the experience of the Holocaust in spite of the difficulties, incongruities and contradictions. Steiner's propositions should not be dismissed in the light of the accumulating literary evidence to the contrary, but should be modified to incorporate the dialectic between language and silence that has emerged in the work of certain writers.

Several critics and writers have assigned generic names to the body of literature that emanated from the Holocaust. In his Foreword to Wiesel's *Night*, Francois Mauriac called it "Lazarene literature" and described what had first drawn him to the young writer: "that look, as of a Lazarus risen from the dead, yet still a prisoner within the grim confines where he had strayed, stumbling among the shameful corpses". In attempting to understand the events of the Holocaust, and having, as he admitted then, no knowledge of Nazi methods of extermination, Mauriac felt that the young Wiesel "may have resembled him – the Crucified, whose Cross had conquered the world". He maintains: "The Jewish nation had been resurrected from among its thousands of dead".

This Christological approach has been expounded by Harry James Cargas in his book, *In Conversation with Elie Wiesel*: "Lazarene literature, that product of confinement, is increasingly being recognised as an important genre of writing. It is truly the literature of resurrection". He maintains that currently it is the political prisoners who are occupying the role of literary Lazaruses and cites Alexander Solzhenitsyn's *One Day in the Life of Ivan Denisovich* to illustrate his point. Cargas also names other writers in this genre: Horst Bienek, Phillip and Daniel Berrigan, Arthur Koestler, David Rousset, Robert Antheleme, Dostoyevski, St John of the Cross, Oscar Wilde and St Paul. He includes Elie Wiesel in his list of authors, claiming that with *Night* Wiesel "takes his place with the best of these writers," this book being "a supreme representation of a whole sub-genre of literature which can be labelled under the heading of Holocaust Literature". While Cargas's scholarship has contributed greatly to a wider acceptance of the literary value of Wiesel's works, his classification is misleading. The term "Lazarene" implies an overtly Christian concept of resurrection which cannot appropriately be applied to the Jewish experience about which Wiesel writes, nor should Auschwitz be likened to concentration camps in Soviet Russia, incarceration in Siberia, confinement in the prisons and camps during World War 1 or the Spanish Civil War. Moreover, there is a qualitative difference in the way in which the surviving witnesses of Auschwitz bear testimony in their literature.

In *The Holocaust and the Literary Imagination*, Lawrence Langer examines Rousset's concept of *l'univers concentrationnaire*, the realm of the concentration camps, which Rousset maintains is known only to the concentrationees: "They are set apart from the rest of the world by an experience impossible to communicate". Through his study of fifteen major writers of this period, Langer attempts to show the improbabilities and impenetrability of this universe. By selecting a representative body of poetry and prose, he illustrates the way in which writers have devised an idiom and a style for the unspeakable that illuminate the recurrent themes of the tradition of atrocity:

> The aesthetic problem of reconciling normalcy with horror: the displacement of the consciousness of life by imminence and pervasiveness of death; the violation of the coherence of childhood; the assault on physical reality; and the disruption of chronological time. (xii)

Langer offers the view that before 1939 imagination was always in advance of reality, but that after 1945 reality had outdistanced the imagination, so that "nothing the artist conjured up could equal in intensity and scope of the improbabilities of *l'univers concentrationnaire*". Langer notes that as early as 1946 a young German writer, Wolfgang Borchert, was tormented with the question:

"After such horrors, what language?" In a lyrical essay entitled "In May, In May Cried the Cuckoo," Borchert wrote: "We must make a note of our misery" with two hundred printed pages serving as a commentary on "the twenty thousand invisible pages on the Sisyphus pages which make up our life, for which we know no words, no grammar and no punctuation" (quoted in Langer, *The Holocaust and the Literary Imagination*). Ironically, while demanding the most heroic deed from the poets, to "Be silent!", Borchert was himself searching for a means to tell his story.[1]

From his extensive research into the literature inspired by the Holocaust, Langer proposes that there is indeed an "aesthetics of atrocity," which, "however hesitantly," he compares to Aristotle's principles of drama that grew into a poetics and a foundation for literary criticism. The name he gives to this body of writing is "the literature of atrocity". He perceives that the task of the artist is to find a style and a form to "present the atmosphere or landscape of atrocity, to make it compelling, to coax the reader into credulity – and ultimately, complicity". In developing his notion of an aesthetics of atrocity, Langer in his subsequent book, *The Age of Atrocity*, is concerned with the evolution of the idea of atrocity in the twentieth century. He limits the scope of his study to the gradual erosion of the human image, as shown by writers to major traumas of our time: Thomas Mann to World War 1, Albert Camus to World War 2, Alexander Solzhenitsyn to Soviet labour camps and Charlotte Delbo to Nazi extermination camps. In choosing these authors for his central study, and in citing many others concerned with the phenomenon of mass atrocity and "inappropriate death", Langer is attempting to broaden the base of his investigation into the literature of atrocity by comparing and contrasting imaginative works, finding parallels between authors and their subject matter, discovering common psychological implications and establishing historical and political antecedents for mass execution. He quotes extensively from Robert Jay Lifton's book *Death in Life*, maintaining that although Lifton is describing the Hiroshima experience, there are sufficient allusions to the concentration camp ordeal to "convince us, that despite the radical differences in the instruments and manner of death, Auschwitz and Hiroshima are twin expressions of a human and technological will to destruction, and we are all survivors of atrocity".(60)

Langer's comparative study of the literary responses to experiences of atrocity has the advantage of dealing critically with literature that shares the common goal of expressing imaginatively the intolerable reality of our modern era. However, I believe that his proposed genre of the literature of atrocity, as with Cargas's classification of Lazarene literature, is too generalised for the particular literary responses that emerged from the unique experience of the Holocaust. This literature should have its own specific generic classification. An appropriate name for this literature is suggested by Wiesel himself in *Dimensions of the Holocaust*:

> If the Greeks invented tragedy, the Romans the epistle, and the Renaissance the sonnet, our generation invented a new literature, that of testimony. We have all been witnesses and we feel we have to bear testimony for the future.(9)

The literature of testimony is indeed a special inheritance of the Holocaust, affirming the dilemma of the writer attempting to describe the indescribable. The distinguishing feature of this genre is the obsession to bear witness to the incommunicable experience of Auschwitz.

The approach I have chose for my study is to analyse the narrative techniques in Wiesel's fiction, with particular emphasis on the role of the narrator and listener in the narratives. This will not only highlight aspects of his authorial strategy involving the reader's response to various dimensions of the Holocaust, but will allow an appraisal of the literary merit of Wiesel's novels. The hushed reverence that tends to accompany allusions to Auschwitz and its literature has impeded certain theoretical investigations, with the result that most critical studies undertaken on Wiesel's works have dealt predominantly with themes and content rather than with form. A narrative approach, however, while it accounts for themes, does so within the narrative process of the work. Form and content are examined as interwoven entities in the particular context of an individual work. My decision to adopt this pursuit is based on the conviction that Wiesel's fiction is a significant contribution to the literature of testimony, not only because of its subject matter, but also because of the way in which his narrators unfold their stories with words suspended by silence in the text.

The mute narrator is intended to convey the paradoxical quality of Wiesel's fiction and to show how silence, which is manifested in the themes of his work, is concretised by his strategy of entrusting the transmission of the tale to narrators, who, for various reasons have been silenced. A mute by definition cannot emit an articulate sound. A narrator, on the other hand, is a storyteller who is reliant on verbal articulation for communication. This contradiction in terms is dramatised in the novels and is symptomatic of the dilemma of Wiesel's narrators who are compelled to bear testimony through their silence.

Wiesel's distinction as a serious contemporary novelist

becomes apparent when the reader's expectations from a story that cannot be told are realised through its telling. His authorial strategies in handling his subject matter have created his own fictional universe. As an author in the literature of testimony, he has achieved a balance between language and silence.

In my study of Wiesel's fiction, I will follow the chronological sequence in which the novels were written, although I will not be using a developmental approach, except to point out that the trilogy which marks the beginning of his exploration into narrative strategies, and *The Testament*, the last book I will be dealing with, are a culmination of his previous fictional techniques. While a developmental analysis of his fiction, particularly from a thematic point of view, enables the reader to gain insight into his background, which is important in a comprehensive study of his works, I feel that this avenue of investigation has been competently dealt with by other critics. Ellen Fine's *Legacy of Night*, one of the first book-length studies of Wiesel, puts forward a convincing argument for examining his fiction in chronological sequence as a kind of serialised journey from being a witness in *l'univers concentrationnaire* to bearing witness in a post-Holocaust world. Furthermore, it is possible to trace the direction Wiesel's fiction follows, as in each book the seeds are sown for new ideas which are expanded upon in subsequent books.

My discussion, however, will deal with the narrative process of each novel as an individual work in its own particular context. Apart from the trilogy which is examined in one chapter, and *The Testament* which serves as a conclusion to the study, I have attempted to not use cross references to Wiesel's other fiction when analysing specific books. Moreover, I have deliberately avoided including Wiesel's comments on his works and references to them in his essays, interviews and non-fiction writing. The reason for this approach is that I consider each novel to be a separate narrative work which merits an interpretative response that is independent of the comparative criteria that has up to now influenced the assessment of his fiction.

CHAPTER 1
CRITICAL RESPONSES TO WIESEL'S WRITINGS AND AN EVALUATION OF HIS NARRATIVE STRATEGIES

"One is not a writer for having to say certain things," Sartre maintains, "but for having chosen to say them in a certain way." In order to further illuminate his novels, I wish to focus on the "certain way" in which Wiesel has chosen to say things. In his continual search for ways of telling a story that cannot be told, Wiesel has explored almost every possibility of narrative form, thereby creating his own fictional universe. At the core of his writing is the tension between the need to keep silent and the compulsion to speak out. The multifaceted dimensions of silence and its inherent paradoxes are the matrix of his narrative art. In his novels, Wiesel attempts to initiate the reader into the realm of silence, to coax the listener away from being a passive recipient into becoming a teller of tales, in a world of words where silence, too, is a way of saying.

Wiesel's ambivalent attitude towards writing about the Holocaust adds to the paradoxical quality of his works. He says in *Dimensions of the Holocaust*, "One cannot write about the Holocaust. Not if you are a writer". However, all his books are in some way a response to the Holocaust, whether they are his Midrashic, Hasidic, or Talmudic stories, his plays, cantata, novels, essays or dialogues. He is constantly being associated with Holocaust literature, yet he denies there is such a thing, insisting it is a contradiction in terms. His commitment to bear witness as a survivor is as intense as his avoidance of direct description of the physical atrocities of the concentration camp experience.

His open rejection of art for art's sake and the fact that the Holocaust imposed the vocation of a writer upon him, have added to the reluctance on the part of critics to analyse his fiction as narrative art. Wiesel himself seems to invite and even encourage this attitude by his own commentaries on the reasons why he is compelled to write. In *Legends of Our Time* he has defined his writing as an act of commemoration: "for me writing is a 'matzeva', an invisible tombstone erected to the memory of the dead unburied". However, a tombstone is not a literary genre. Having written to date some 25 books in a variety of literary modes, Wiesel still claims he is not a novelist or essayist, but a vehicle, a messenger to the unburied dead. It is not surprising, therefore, that the critics have been more concerned with the messenger and the message than the way in which the message is delivered. Wiesel's attitude towards his vocation as a writer creates almost insurmountable obstacles for the critic concerned with his work as literature rather than as a personal validation of events by a survivor. It should however be remembered that although the Holocaust is at the core of his experience and has determined his philosophy, it is always on the periphery of his novels.

As a survivor and witness he has been accorded respect bordering on reverence. As a man, teacher and interpreter of Biblical, Talmudic, Midrashic and Hasidic tales, both Jewish and Christian scholars have acclaimed his wisdom as a contemporary prophet-teacher and transmitter of tradition. one critic, Arthur A. Cohen, who calls him the master of the Holocaust, in his article "Silence and Laughter" has said, "He is more than all the extraordinary documents which have come out of that period, the rediscovered journals and diaries, the narrative accounts and reconstructions". And yet, Wiesel has been granted little recognition as a writer of contemporary fiction and the critical commentary on his work as literature attests to the notion that his subject matter takes precedence over his "way of saying."

Most of the commentaries on Wiesel's work, particularly his fiction, are based on the moral, philosophical and theological implications contained in the questions he poses. They are questions pertaining to God's absence in the Holocaust, a post-Holocaust future in accordance with a pre-Holocaust past of faith, the possible redemption and regeneration of mankind through a changed vision of God, man and the universe. Because the theological dialectic is at the core of his narrative art, Carol P. Christ calls his mode of writing "story theology", maintaining that the theology cannot be abstracted from the narrative. This view seems to be favoured by the majority of critics in *Responses to Elie Wiesel*, a book of collected critical essays by major Jewish and Christian scholars. Here the emphasis is placed on the theological content and subject matter of his writing, rather than on literary considerations. Maurice Friedman calls him "the Job of Auschwitz", Michael Berenbaum regards him as "the Theologian of the Void" and has written a book by that title, Byron Sherwin acknowledges that he is "the high priest of our generation", and Robert Alter assesses his novels as being "more theological parable than realistic fiction". Ted Estess, asserting that Wiesel's work is parabolic and elliptical, feels he is attempting to provide "an ideationally significant response to painful religious, social and psychological dilemmas". In the last essay of this book, the editor, Harry James Cargas, offers extracts from letters and published writings by leading Christian theologians, scholars and teachers, showing the significant influence of Wiesel's writing on contemporary Christian religious life and thought. The intention of Cargas's survey is to show how Wiesel's testimony has forced religious thinkers to confront the Holocaust with a new awareness of the reality of evil, suffering and death, while reaffirming a life of faith through the Hasidic tradition of a dialogue with God.

Cargas quotes from a letter by Father Malcolm Boyd which seems to encapsulate the sentiments of other writers:

> Wiesel's is the dominant contemporary voice and
> presence that impinges ever anew upon my awareness of
> it, opening upon my awareness of it, opening up new
> dimensions of the Holocaust for me; reminding me again
> and again when I might seek to relax the tautness of my
> hold on my spirit; and telling me quite simply that the
> agony of the Holocaust is embedded beneath the facade
> of our resolutely smiling, outwardly secure, wilfully
> complacent, self absorbed caricature of life that is
> conveniently labelled 'Christian.' (289)

Until now, the book-length studies on Wiesel's writings have in fact mainly been carried out by Christian scholars and theologians who are largely responsible for the upsurge of interest in Wiesel. A recently published book by a leading Protestant theologian and teacher, Robert McAfee Brown, dealing with the personal, ecumenical and philosophical aspects of Wiesel's work, appeared under the title *Elie Wiesel: Messenger to All Humanity*. Indeed his voice is reaching a larger and larger audience. A lengthy article devoted to Wiesel's life and work in *The New York Times Magazine* has recognised Wiesel as one of the most well known Jews in the United States, particularly as a teacher and lecturer.

Wiesel's "moral authority", his "prophetic witness", his role as messenger to humanity, his contributions towards writing a new Midrash, as well as reviving Lamentation literature, have been expounded fairly extensively by the critics. On the other hand, the literary value of his narrative art has received little attention. It is the opinion of many literary critics that Wiesel's novels are significant but are not novels of "great style." However, if style is conceived as a value term, as it is in this context, it is a measure of accomplishment that is relevant to understanding both art and culture as a whole. The term "style" can usually be used with confidence as an independent clue to the time and origin of a work of art. In a. collected volume of essays, *Aesthetics Today*, an interesting definition of style has been offered by Meyer Schapiro:

> The style is, above all, a system of forms with a quality and a meaningful expression through which the personality of the artist and the broad outlook of the group are visible . . . It is, besides, a common ground against which innovations and the individuality of particular works may be measured. (156)

This definition is especially apt when assessing individual novels in Wiesel's fictional universe and measuring them against the background of his Hasidic tradition and Holocaust experience. While his style is distinct from that of contemporary Jewish novelists such as, Saul Bellow, Bernard Malamud and Isaac Bashevis Singer, it does reflect certain features of his cultural background, the personality of Wiesel, the artist, and "the broad outlook of the group." Wiesel's style, therefore, should be evaluated in the light of Schapiro's definition rather than on a comparative basis with modern American novelists.

In advocating an alternative critical approach to Wiesel's fiction, further criteria must be established that take into account his narrative strategies which determine the structural organisation of particular works. The most significant features in his fiction are the interrelationship between narrator and listener, the use of tense to combine past and present time, the spatial perspective that distances and narrows narrative focus and the techniques and devices used to evoke silence. A crucial and innovative narrative device in Wiesel's novels is the paradox of the mute narrator. Often the most powerful response evoked from the reader results not only from what Wiesel's narrators leave unsaid but from the silence that is imposed on them, whether they happen to be mute or are compelled not to speak. Wiesel uses silence as an artistic strategy and as Terence Des Pres points out in *Confronting the Holocaust*, silence is "an effective solution to an aesthetic problem", the problem of meaning and communication.

It has been acknowledged that Wiesel is easy to read but difficult to assimilate. The simplicity of his use of language often disguises the complexity of thought and intention. The reader is required to bear the burden that involves a change of consciousness, a re-evaluation of pre-conceived notions, a shift in modes of perception and furthermore, an acceptance of knowledge that could only rationally be applied to an absurd world of inverted values. Frans Kafka presented to his readers a universe of absurd and frightening proportions, and although "In The Penal Settlement" is a fictional and ordered world, and as such cannot be compared to the Holocaust universe, there are many elements that are considered to be uncanny prefigurations of *l'univers concentrationnaire*. Moreover, it was Kafka's conviction that:

> We must have those books which come upon us like ill fortune, and distress us deeply, like the death of one we love better than ourselves, like suicide. A book must be an ice-axe to break the sea frozen inside us."(excerpted in Steiner, *Language and Silence* (90)

A similar response to Wiesel's writing is quoted by Cargas in *Responses to Elie Wiesel*: "Wiesel's work has often been like a fingernail drawn across the full length of a blackboard in my consciousness; an almost unbearable presence, sound and effect being brought to bear on my deepest feelings and conscience."

It can be argued that the reader should not be required to carry the burden of guilt and share the role of witness that the author imposes on himself. It should be possible to read, interpret, analyse and compare a work of fiction in the genre of testimony with other fictional works without having to place it in the particular context of the anti-world of the Holocaust. In *Confronting the Holocaust*, Alvin Rosenfeld remarks: "In the ghettos and camps of Europe, 'reality' underwent so radical a distortion", that the possibility and validity of a literature of the Holocaust seemed destined to commit a grave injustice against the victims. The tradition that preceded it was hopelessly out of touch with its subject. A writer, confronting a subject that threatened to overwhelm the resources of language, could no longer rely on the established literary forms of the past. The conception of man and his world expressed in the major writings of our literary tradition lacked validity in a world where the most extreme imaginings had to be perceived as the actual event.

The proposition that the Holocaust is without likeness or kind leads to the implication that its literature is without antecedents or analogy, without metaphor, simile or symbol. Rosenfeld argues that one of the most distinguishing characteristics of Holocaust literature, and "what may be one if its abiding laws", is that "there are no metaphors for Auschwitz, just as Auschwitz is not a metaphor for anything else."[2] Many writers and scholars attempt to find analogies in the Bible, in history, in cosmic disasters and catastrophes, and even in the atrocities and massacres perpetrated in our time. Yet, they only reveal their inadequacy and inappropriateness. The poet Uri Zvi Greenberg expresses this view in his poem "We were not likened to Dogs among Gentiles":

> Are there analogies to this, our disaster that came upon
> us at their hands?
> There are no analogies (all words are shades of shadow)
> Therein lies the horrifying phrase: No other analogies!
> (excerpted in Rosenfeld (12))

In the introduction to his study *A Double Dying: Reflections on Holocaust Literature*, Rosenfeld points out that even though this special corpus greatly complicates existing literary forms – and even breaks them down in its effort to express the Holocaust – it has finally "not occasioned any new kinds of writing." In his article, "Believing in Holocaust Literature", James E. Young supports this conclusion by stating: "Perhaps we all expected a startling new literary form to emerge from the shattered sensibilities of the Holocaust", an experience that would surely provoke its artists and writers to new aesthetic modes and innovations. Instead, Young believes the Holocaust has forced readers and critics to adjust their conceptions of art and literature. In contrast to this opinion, I would argue that if an adjustment is forced on the reader and critic, it is precisely because the literary form provokes a changed response and a new consciousness of a literature that has no analogies. The literature of testimony does in fact testify to the impossibility of its task. It continually impinges on the critical dialectic of whether there can be an aesthetic code to express the inexpressible. If the writer's credibility is dependent on the inadequacy of language to describe the most extreme imaginings, then the reader must not only be willing to "suspend disbelief," but be prepared to accept the silence in the text as part of the reading process required for this genre. The changes that occur in the interrelations between writer, narrator, reader and subject matter through the organizing principles of narration, have initiated narrative innovations and do provoke "new" and participatory responses in the reader.

The participation of the reader in works of fiction in this genre leads to the question of the eligibility of the writer. Is it only those who wrote and died in Auschwitz, and now is it only those who survived who can tell the tale? Wiesel's position seems to be unequivocal on this issue. He has repeatedly stated that whoever has not lived through the event can never know it, and whoever has lived through it can never fully reveal it. He believes that a survivor's testimony is more important than anything that can be written by others. Nevertheless, although Wiesel and many survivor poets, novelists, dramatists and diarists have created the literature of testimony, there have been other writers, such as Terence Des Prez, Edward Alexander, André Neher and George Steiner who feel they can no longer "dare not to speak." They have respected the sentiments of Wiesel and other survivors not to betray the dead. It must, therefore, be acknowledged that the writers-who are-not-survivors, "the non-inhabitants of the death camps," have contributed greatly to an understanding of the dimensions of the Holocaust. Critics such as Lawrence Langer, Alvin Rosenfeld, Sidra DeKoven Ezrahai and many others, have explored the crucial role of this literature and have examined a range of texts that may not otherwise have been brought to light for critical evaluation. On the other hand, as the subject of the Holocaust creates more and more interest, and is now used readily as a background for best selling novels and commercially viable films, survivors-turned-writers, as well as popular fiction writers, are exploiting an event after almost four decades of silence.[3] Once taboo, the theme has become a popular commodity for horror and sensationalism. Even though these survivors often offer evidence of their survival by recalling episodes of their concentration camp experience, they are not writing in the genre of the literature of testimony. The touchstone for the adequacy of literary works as testimony must be discerned through the narrative strategies, including the use of silence, that provoke a different kind of perspective and response from the reader. It is not through the subject matter that the meaning of the story becomes apparent, but through the way in which the story is told.

The difficulties inherent in telling a tale as testimony in Wiesel's fiction are manifested through his presentation of the silent, invisible or mute narrators and their listeners.

His narrators not only question the capacity of language to render truth, but challenge the ability of the individual to convey a story without distorting fictional reality. One of Wiesel's distinctive narrative devices is for several narrators to tell the same story in a variety of ways, which allow it to be seen from alternative perspectives. This device permits a doubt, not as to the facts, but as to the validity of a single interpretation. While the multiple narrative voices complicate and fragment the narration, they also serve as a strategy to increase the narrative distance in the novels. This makes it possible for the reader to make interpretative responses to each version of the story and each change in the mode of perception demanded by the new narrator.

Wiesel's narrators emerge unannounced from the past, intrude into the present and often foreshadow the future. They are purposely vague, mystical and elusive figures, having no distinguishing characteristics. They may be old or young, but never of a specific age; they may have a name which is the name of another; they appear, disappear and then reappear in a different guise; they have no distinctive life of their own, nor do they have a recognisable family or a particular social environment. They cannot be easily identified from either their physical appearance or any emotional or psychological qualities. They are beggars, madmen, wanderers, teachers, story tellers and messengers. They are often a combination of characters with numerous voices; some arrive from the distant and legendary past, while others rise from the midst of the unburied dead or are the progeny of the present.

The lack of characterisation in Wiesel's fiction, with the possible exception of his seventh novel, *The Testament*, is a major clue to his narrative strategy. A similar feature in Kafka's writing has been noted by Marthe Robert in her

book *Frans Kafka's Loneliness*:
> Unlike all other known figures in novels, the typical character in Kafka is without attraction of any kind; nor is he calculated to arouse interest; he is distinguished by no winning trait, by no psychological subtlety, by no faculty for inspiring passions and ideas, this denuding is deliberate. Lacking most of the characteristics that ordinarily attach to the fictitious characters of novels, without distinctive physical traits or moral qualities, he fascinates solely by the inexplicable gaps in the characterisation, which makes him not an identified person but an obsessive enigma, hence a constant stimulant to thought. (6)

In spite of the curiously abstract quality of Kafka's heroes, he is primarily concerned with the image of modern man which for him, as Maurice Friedman in *Problematic Rebel* states, is "nothing less than the meaning of human existence face to face with the absurd". His writings cannot be reduced to abstract philosophical concepts, or religious, political or sociological allegories or parables pointing to universal truth. Kafka's understanding of the term "artist" is, "the man who expresses the inexpressible, who defines what cannot be defined, who sees and sets forth aspects and inner realities of our concrete existence that most people are not aware of or cannot express" (Friedman, 388).

As a writer, Kafka could not divorce his art from his existence and establish it as a separate realm of meaning and value. Neither could he leave his life out of his art, since he believed that "art is always a matter of entire personality." It is my suggestion that Wiesel's writing, too, is a matter of entire personality. Wiesel's claim that his life is a commentary on his books, "not the other way around," suggests to an extent that his vocation as a writer was thrust upon him as a survivor and witness, and not out of choice. It can also be construed as a rationale for his denial that he is a novelist. But it is not a question of whether his books are a commentary on his life, or that his life is a commentary on his books – both arguments apply. The either/or dialectic serves only to place emphasis on the part rather than the whole. The life/art debate should be replaced by a life and art appraisal, the interlacing of vocation and literary achievement. It is only in his writing that the meaning of survival, and his paradoxical and often contradictory relation to it, can be established.

The enigmatic quality of Wiesel's narrators and the thin dividing line between the narrators and Wiesel himself is a contentious issue for the literary evaluation of his novels. The intrusion of the author's voice, often in misplaced aphorisms or authorial sermons, disturbs the organisational principles of the novel, increases the fragmentation of the narration and reduces the narrative focus of the reader. This has been seen as a lapse in Wiesel's style and has led to the view held by Geoffrey Hartman that "if you separated the fiction from the man, they wouldn't have the same impact" (quoted. in *The New York Times Magazine*). It is, however, impossible to separate his works from the one event that is at the core of his writing. Wiesel is a writer and a witness, and his style of narration is part of his message.

While Wiesel's life and art must be considered together, it is nevertheless necessary to separate his own comments on his work from his narrators' points of view. Individual works should be dealt with without resorting to the commentary by the author. In his essays, conversations and interviews, Wiesel often discusses similar themes to the narrators in his novels. Because of the diverse perspectives, the multiple voices, the ambivalent and paradoxical presentation of motifs in a particular novel, often contradicted in another novel, it is frequent critical practice to quote Wiesel outside his art in order to clarify the veiled meaning in his fiction. The conflict that faces the literary critic is that Wiesel's accessibility as a living writer provides the opportunity to verify certain theoretical conclusions by referring directly to the authority of the author. While this approach is often unavoidable, and may be preferable in certain instances, it does tend to distort meaning out of the context in which it is written. This is particularly apparent in Wiesel's fiction which raises questions in a variety of ways and leaves them open-ended. Furthermore, his prolificacy as a writer, his social role and public presence inevitably influence interpretative comment on his narrative art. However, where possible, Wiesel's views should not be used as a substitute for the texts of individual works, particularly as he is often deliberately ambivalent and controversial about what he writes. As a result, the paradoxes which are central to his mode of narration are often reduced to singular statements so that the possibilities of alternative interpretations are lost. Henry James's maxim "never to trust the teller" but "to trust the tale" is a useful formula when dealing with Wiesel's diverse literary forms. A distinction should be made between Wiesel, the teller, and the narrators of his tales. While Wiesel often elucidates a view point, never fully expressed by his narrators in a fictional work, a full understanding of its meaning can only be arrived at by considering the way in which it is presented, who is presenting it and why it is presented in the context of a particular novel. For these reasons, I believe that the narrative strategies are a key to his fiction.

An attitude accepted by many of Wiesel's critics is that

in his fiction the words are more memorable than the characters. While it is true that his characters are never identifiable heroes and may therefore not be remarkable, it is equally true that it is not always the words themselves that are memorable, but the way in which the words are used. Each narrator expresses his own truth in his own voice. This is why cross-references to his poems, plays, and numerous essays do not offer an appropriate alternative to the voices of the narrators in his fiction. Although, for instance, *Ani Maamin* questions the silence of God in Auschwitz and affirms faith "in spite of" the Holocaust, a theme that is explored in most of Wiesel's works, the poem cannot be explained in terms of the essays in *A Jew Today*, nor can it be used as a hopeful conclusion to *The Gates of the Forest*. It must be read and comprehended in its own context.

Similarly, the critical commentaries on *The Town Beyond the Wall* are inevitably drawn from his essay "The Last Return," an account of his journey back to Sighet, which ironically took place two years after the writing of the novel. In the essay, Wiesel himself compares his return with the theme of the novel and writes that he used the book as a guide: "Seen in daylight the town appeared exactly as I had dreamed it: bare without any vigour, without any mystery". Wiesel too, has narrated a television film of his return, entitled "The Itinerary of Elie Wiesel: From Sighet to Jerusalem." He has lectured on the subject and maintained in *Dimension of the Holocaust* that the function of the survivor witness, is precisely "to bring back to life people and places destroyed by the executioner and to prove that Jews can with words, build upon ruins". In the same lecture he explained why the *shtetl*, the little village of Eastern Europe, became the illustration for memoirs: "The *shtetl*, that small kingdom of fire erected and purified in fire, has disappeared for ever . . . it has survived in words alone." The essays and lectures are relevant and instructive as autobiographical explications of the themes of *The Town Beyond the Wall*, but the town in the novel is not Sighet, the fictitious narrator is not Wiesel, nor is the tale the author's story. In this novel, the motif of the spectator has been used as a springboard for theological and philosophical discourses on Wiesel's attitude to the role of the spectator during the Holocaust. McAfee Brown believes that Wiesel's work is completely synonymous with "the moral society" and regards the spectator's "voluntary withdrawal from participation" in *The Town Beyond the Wall*, as "an abdication of personhood" (quoted in *Face to Face*). He concludes that for Wiesel, remaining a spectator is the most morally reprehensible response of all. However, in the novel, the spectator's role is not used as a moral lesson for the reader but is dramatised for narrative purposes. The dramatic confrontation between the spectator and the narrator provides the narrative climax of the story.

For every theme in the novels there is a parallel elsewhere in Wiesel's non-fiction. A study of his essays would reveal a repetitiveness and a sense of urgency in his role as survivor-witness which, at his own insistence, appears to be more crucial than his authorial role. It is precisely because his narrative accounts, stories and essays retell the same story in different forms that the critic is inexorably drawn to them for elucidation in an attempt to "fill in the gaps" of his fictional world. But these literary modes are not in the tradition of the novel. Henry James's definition of the novel is particularly apt as it highlights diverse aspects of the novelist's art:

> The novel . . . reports of an infinite diversity of matters, gathers together and gives out again a hundred sorts, and

finds its order-and its structure, its unity and its beauty in the alteration of parts and the adjustment of differences. ("The New Novel",385)

In studying the form of the novel, one cannot abstract or isolate a particular feature for independent consideration; each element has its relative significance in its relation to the novel's whole configuration of diverse elements. Although one must be concerned with plot, character, setting and theme, they must be seen in relation to the totality of the work. In addition, one must take cognisance of the narrative process, the way in which aspects of the narration interact with one another and are interdependent on each other to create a structural unity.

Many of the recent studies of Wiesel's fiction are thematic analyses, which generally include plot, character and setting. While these elements are important as a background and framework for his novels, they do not take into account the narrative presentation of these themes. In his novels Wiesel not only explores themes in their various manifestations, but he tries out fictional techniques, discards them and adopts new ones, and then finally and deliberately leaves his fiction open-ended. The novels cannot be systematically organised to represent experience because the causes that shape and determine the sequence of events cannot all be known. In that he explores a reality that must finally remain unknown, there is a similarity between his narrative art and Herman Melville's multiplicity of perspectives in *Moby Dick*. Melville believed that human life was part of the inscrutable mysteriousness of God, and that the inscrutable cannot be represented directly. As Richard Brodhead remarks in *Hawthorne, Melville and the Novel*: "As an artist Melville is thus engaged in-the paradoxical task of seeking to make sense of something that he insists from the outset defies comprehension".

It is my assumption that a literary appreciation of Wiesel's fiction should be concerned with the multiple levels of meaning evoked by the various fictional modes of presentation he employs. Critics should not try to eliminate the contradictions and incongruities which are at the core of his writing, nor should they ignore the narrative paradoxes that deliberately suggest something that finally cannot be known. It is not a question of "filling in the gaps," but rather an imperative to become aware of the gaps, the pauses, the lapses of voice, the absence and eclipse of speech and the omission of words. These must be recognised as some of the narrative devices of silence. In the same way, madness, laughter, prayer and song are not only thematic considerations, but constitute alternative narrative strategies to speech, the telling of the story that cannot finally be told. While I feel that the narrative process in Wiesel's fiction is complex and can pretend to no final validity, a reflection on the paradox of the mute narrator can offer a further dimension to his testimony.

CHAPTER 2
SCENIC SILENCE IN *NIGHT, DAWN* AND *THE ACCIDENT*

The emergence of Wiesel's narrative strategies in his fiction is contained in his first three books, *Night, Dawn* and *The Accident*. In these works the seeds are sown for his paradoxical presentation of the device of the mute narrator, which becomes integral to the narrative process of his subsequent fiction. While there are many continuities in the thematic content of the trilogy, and while the narration of each is first-person, there are differences in the form of each work. However, the boundary between autobiography, memoir and fiction are almost indistinguishable. Although the novels following the trilogy are far more complex and skilful, allowing for a diversity of narrative viewpoints and multiple levels of interpretation, nevertheless the first three books are the foundation upon which Wiesel built his fictional universe.

I will examine the works in the trilogy against the backdrop of "scenic silence," a term coined by André Neher, to show how the characters and narrative voices in his early fiction are transformed into narrators and listeners in the succeeding novels. As silence is central to Wiesel's response to the Holocaust, and determines the various ways in which his narratives are presented, Neher, a leading thinker and writer in contemporary Judaism, having examined "the landscape of silence" in the Bible, has further developed the idea in relation to the silence of Auschwitz. In his book *The Exile of the Word*, he calls Wiesel a "diviner of silence," in that Wiesel has detected and tracked down "the least vibration of silence" in the reality of Auschwitz. Neher maintains that Wiesel has not only learned from his literary masters of silence – Kafka, Joyce and Saint-Exupery – but differs with, and surpasses them:

> Ploughed, sown, and reaped within the Kingdom of Silence, the work of Elie Wiesel is permeated with silence, as a fruit is imbued with the soil which nurtured it. It is certainly a theme, and even the word, which appears most often in the text (nearly a thousand times), and a computer would doubtless inform us that no literary creation of the twentieth century evokes silence with such variety, intensity, and diversity as that of Elie Wiesel.(210)

It is Neher's view that in the works of Wiesel, silence has three principle functions. The first is phenomenological, where the silence serves as a kind of counterpoint to the thought it clarifies, explains, criticises and challenges. The second function, he calls "scenic silence," which serves as a backdrop to the action, "whether dramatic, or lyrical, realistic or mystical, anecdotal or simply imaginary". Theological silence is the third function he examines in Wiesel's work, since he maintains that by bringing the silence of God into the general domain of silence, it has the effect of reversing all religiously established values: "Now it is no longer only the words of men which are submitted to the test of truth, but the word of God".

Neher's proposition encompasses many facets of silence in Wiesel's work, although, Sidra Ezrahi, in her critical study *By Words Alone*, maintains that Neher's approach in paying such homage to silence "is perilous insofar as it assigns meaning to the inarticulate and consequence to the unexpressed". Yet the inarticulate voices and the unexpressed experiences of Wiesel's narrators are by far the most powerful evocation of the testimonial imperative in Wiesel's fiction. However, the function of silence, **what** it does, needs further exploration to show **how** Wiesel uses silence as a narrative device. Not only do "the mute heroes," representing the six million dead, inhabit Wiesel's fictional world "with a prodigality hitherto unprecedented in literature", but the mute narrators and the mute listeners, who bear testimony for the silent dead, must be accounted for in the narrative process of telling their tale. While the roles of narrator and listener are not developed to a significant degree in the trilogy, it is nevertheless possible to show how scenic silence is absorbed into the texts of these early works and used as a narrative technique to give credence to the narration.

After a decade of silence as a survivor of Auschwitz, Wiesel wrote his first book in Yiddish. Directly translated its title would be *And the World was Silent*. Two years later, he rewrote it in French, condensing the volume of over 300 pages into a third of its original length. It was published as

La Nuit in France, and in 1960 appeared in the English version, *Night*. The shift from Yiddish to French was significant in terms of the way in which he wanted to present his testimony, and having written his first book, the others followed in quick succession. In French, his adopted language, Wiesel was able to use words and images which for him were not weighed down with values from a lost past. In both the prose and dialogues of the book, the sparse, tightly controlled use of language leaves sufficient gaps in the narration for the words, which are not written or spoken, to carry the impact of the silence of Auschwitz.

The critical commentary surrounding *Night*, particularly that of Wiesel in his essays and other writings, inflicts a moral dilemma on the commentator, as literary criticism is considered a disservice, even an act of betrayal to the content of the work. McAfee Brown, in *Elie Wiesel: Messenger to All Humanity*, expresses an opinion shared by many critics: "Of all Wiesel's works, *Night* is the one that most cries out not to be touched, interpreted, synthesised". In tracing "The Journey into Night," in *Elie Wiesel*, Ted Estess maintains that one is reluctant to apply the usual conventions of literary analysis to the book since it would blunt the impact of its testimony: "Against the horror of the story, literary considerations seem somehow beside the point. And in a real sense they are, for Wiesel's principal concern is not literary". Wiesel, himself has declared that every word in the book is true, insisting that the story must be read in the light of this statement. He recently said in an interview with Ellen Fine in *Centerpoint*: "If I had to write it today, it would be the same. I would use the same words and speak the same way". He has repeatedly asserted that *Night* is the foundation of his work; all the rest is commentary. In agreement with other critics in *Responses to Elie Wiesel*, Irving Halperin believes that Wiesel is an important writer, not by the rules of contemporary fiction, but because his books "excite us to intense reflection" and suggest "some of the most crucial, if unanswerable questions pertinent to the Holocaust.

While in *Night* Wiesel poses questions about the Holocaust, which are indeed crucial and unanswerable, the questions still arise as to why *Night* defies interpretation except on a moral and theological level. Why does the book evoke such horror and "excite us to intense reflection?" It is not only the subject matter: there have been countless documents, memoirs, diaries and fictional works that have given more graphic and horrifying accounts of the Holocaust Kingdom, yet they have not had the same influence, nor aroused the "reader's agony" and moral anger to the same degree. Wiesel is not the only survivor to have written the story, but he is the only survivor to have written it in the way he has. The authorial choice was his: the words he chose, the form he created, the modes of narration he explored, the narrative techniques he used to structure the work, attest to a literary art. The subject matter of *Night* is an intimidating challenge to the critic, but the approach which consciously avoids a confrontation with the literature born of the "monstrous evil" that was Auschwitz, denies the literary value of works in the literature of testimony.

Although *Night* is strongly autobiographical, Wiesel uses various novelistic devices that combine the immediacy of autobiographical narration with the perspective and distance of a first-person novel. At no time does he fictionalise the experience, nor is the reader left in doubt that the represented world of the Kingdom of Night is real. As Barbara Foley notes, the hallucinatory atmosphere "of the full grotesqueness of life and death in Auschwitz" created through the narrative process, "invests his memoir with some of the symbolic dimensions of a full-fledged fiction."(341)

The book begins with a description of Mochè the Beadle, a character who reappears in almost all Wiesel's fiction. In subsequent novels, he is often presented as a beadle in a synagogue, arriving in the narrator's home town from nowhere and disappearing to an unknown destination. He is usually portrayed as a madman and a messenger, bearing a message from the dead to the living. His role is also that of a teacher who transmits his knowledge and wisdom of the traditional past, opening the gates of Jewish mysticism to his disciple and listener, the narrator of the tale. His presence in the story is significant, not only in relation to the narrator's past, but in terms of the narrative process. Mochè the Beadle, in all his fictional guises, is always a storyteller.

In *Night*, Mochè's appearance is a prelude to the memoir and provides it with a strange, unreal prefiguration of events that follow his disappearance after his prophetic message to the community of the impending massacre of the Jews. As in most of Wiesel's subsequent fiction, the portrait of Mochè is sketched with no definitive lines and is left incomplete:

> They called him Mochè the Beadle, as though he had
> never had a surname in his life. He was a man of all work
> at a Hasidic synagogue . . . . Nobody ever felt encumbered
> by his presence. He was a past master in the art of making
> himself insignificant, of seeming invisible. (12)

As with Moishe the Madman in *The Town Beyond the Wall*, Mochè the Beadle speaks little, preferring to sing. In their dialogues with the narrators, Michael and Eliezer, it is apparent that the madness of both men stems from the absurdity of the world in which they live, and of which they cannot speak. Mochè the Beadle becomes mad after his miraculous escape from the Gestapo, who took him for dead, when the foreign Jews, having dug their own graves, were shot in a forest. He returns to the *shtetl* to tell the story to the community and warn them of their impending fate. Through long days and nights he goes from house to house telling the story of Malka, "the young girl who had taken three days to die," and of Tobias the tailor, "who had begged to be killed before his sons". Mochè no longer sings or speaks of God and the Kabbalah; he only tells stories of what he has seen. But the community, taking him for a madman, "refused not only to believe his stories, but even to listen to them". In *Night* Wiesel does not give Mochè a narrative voice except in his brief dialogues with Eliezer. Mochè's stories are told indirectly by the narrator, and only in his later fiction does Wiesel present him as a storyteller. Furthermore, there is no listener in the memoir; even Eliezer does not believe Mochè's stories.

Wiesel further develops the role of Moshe the Beadle in *The Gates of the Forest*. Gavriel, believing that Moshe is the Messiah who could change the world, only acknowledges him as a friend when Moshe's tongue is cut out and he is no longer able to speak. Like Mochè in *Night*, Moshe sings and weeps while he prays, but while Eliezer believes that Mochè will draw him into eternity, Gavriel is blinded by his presence and haunted by his absence in the world in which he lives. While the configuration of the madman changes and evolves in the novels following *Night*, his role is that of a messenger to bear witness for the dead. In *The Oath*, however, Wiesel reverses this role, and Moshe the madman, who is the pivotal narrator of the tale, denounces the right of the survivor to testify. It is perhaps ironical that the introduction of the character Moshe the Beadle in the opening paragraph of *Night* not only initiates Wiesel's fictional universe, but as a first version of Moshe in *The Oath*, he comes full circle, finally accepting the futility of bearing testimony. Just as Mochè in *Night* remains silent, having grown weary of speaking without being heard or understood, so Moshe the madman in *The Oath* is the advocate of silence as testimony.

The first-person narrator Eliezer, the youth Wiesel remembers himself to be, writes of his adolescent experience at Auschwitz from the mature judgement of a survivor. The narrator is distanced from the author, not only in name, but in time and place. The shift in the temporal and spatial orientation of the memoir is achieved by the way in which Wiesel marks the passage of time. In Chapter 1, which briefly spans the period from the end of 1941 until the Spring of 1944, when the Jews are deported from Sighet, time is measured in years. After the deportation of the foreign Jews from the town, time passes in months, weeks and days. Only when the Jews are forced into the convoy of cattle wagons, is time measured in nights. Thereafter the word "night" is evoked with a repetitiveness that comes to symbolise a world filled with flames and death:

> Never shall I forget that night, the first night in the camp, which has turned my life into one long night, seven times cursed and seven times sealed. Never shall I forget that smoke. Never shall I forget the little faces of the children, whose bodies I saw turned into wreaths of smoke beneath a silent blue sky.
> Never shall I forget those flames which consumed my faith forever. (44)

The word "silence" recurs with the same frequency in the text as the word "night," and the two words, and their various associations, become almost synonymous. The Kingdom of Night is silence, and the silence of Auschwitz is night. This equation is not only one of the themes in the book but forms part of the narrative process. The written word leaves space for the unspoken word, and it is left for the reader to decipher the implications in the gaps, the pauses, the fragmented phrases and sentences, and the disjointed images. The scenic silence is apparent in the description of the narrator's landscape as the community prepares to leave Sighet. The scene is crowded with objects but devoid of life and people:

> The street was like a marketplace that had suddenly been abandoned. Everything could be found there: suitcases, portfolios, briefcases, knives, plates, banknotes, papers, faded portraits . . . .
>
> Everywhere rooms lay open. Doors and windows gaped onto the emptiness. Everything was free for anyone, belonging to nobody. It was simply a matter of helping oneself. An open tomb.
>
> A hot summer sun.(27)

The phrases "an open tomb" and "a hot summer sun" are substitutes for complete sentences, and are used as full descriptive statements. Silence precedes and follows them.

In direct contrast to the silence of the empty town, the scene of the march from Buna to Buchenwald is filled with the icy silence of death. The landscape is filled by men "crushed, trampled underfoot, dying", to whom no one pays attention:

> We were outside. The icy wind stung my face. I bit my lips continually to prevent them from freezing. Around me everything was dancing a dance of death. It made my head reel. I was walking in a cemetery, among stiffened corpses, logs of wood. Not a cry of distress, not a groan,

nothing but mass agony, in silence. No one asked anyone else for help. You died because you had to die. There was no fuss. (101)

Having witnessed so many deaths at Auschwitz and Buna, the narrator's perception of death is radically altered on the journey to Buchenwald. Corpses and silence pervade his environment; even natural phenomena dance "a dance of death." The reader becomes aware of the horror of this scene, not only because men were dying on the march, but because of the inevitability and finality of death in a world where there is "nothing but mass agony." The pauses between the sentences, and the void between the words "nothing" and "no one," carry the silence.

By its very nature night is silent, yet in the camp at Buna, Eliezer discovers a unique night sound. A fragment of Beethoven's violin concerto permeates the silence of the camp, purifying the night. Its echo is a reminder of silence that was once sacred:

> It was pitch dark. I could hear only the violin, and it was as though Juliek's soul were the bow. He was playing his life. The whole of his life was gliding on the strings – his lost hopes, his charred past, his extinguished future. He played as he would never play again. (107)

Juliek's audience is comprised of dead and dying men. After his recital, he too died: "Near him lay his violin, smashed, trampled, a strange overwhelming little corpse". The image of the violin, an instrument of sound, being silenced forever, and cast aside as another corpse, evokes the silence of soundless death in the camp. With this story, the narrator shifts the narrative focus from the immediacy of listening to the sound of the violin in the camp, to the time of writing his memoir a decade later. He remarks that, "to this day," whenever he hears the music of Beethoven, he remembers the sad face of his Polish friend, "as he said farewell on his violin to an audience of dying men".

After his father dies in Buchenwald, Eliezer says: "I have nothing to say of my life during this period". The last few pages of the memoir, dealing with the liberation of the inmates, are narrated as short factual statements in a journal report. The liberation is described in terms of appeasing their hunger. The survivors thought of: "Nothing but bread". Again, a phrase must suffice as the only explanation the narrator is prepared to offer the reader. The enormity of Eliezer's unexpressed experience is implied in the last two sentences of the book, when he looks at himself in a mirror:

> From the depths of the mirror, a corpse gazed back at me.
> The look in his eyes, as they stared into mine, has never left me. (127)

Dawn is considered by many critics to be a continuation of *Night*, particularly because of the development of themes suggested by the French titles of the trilogy: *La Nuit*, *L'Aube* and *Le Jour*. Elisha, the narrator of *Dawn*, is thought to be an older version of Eliezer, being a survivor of Auschwitz and continually haunted by the silent dead. While Wiesel has based the story on biographical and historical facts, and the narrative techniques are similar to those used in *Night*, *Dawn* should be assessed as a work of apprenticeship. It is not only Wiesel's first fully fictional work, but it is his only novel in which the dramatic action dominates the narrative process. In spite of its taut prose, unembellished dialogue and gripping story, Wiesel's characteristic handling of the role of the narrator is not yet developed in *Dawn*, nor is the relationship between author, narrator and reader established. Yet, according to the view held by Frederick Garber in his article on "The Art of Elie Wiesel," it is precisely because Wiesel shifts "the order of commentary from the narrator's relation to the reader into the hero's relation to himself", that he considers *Dawn* to be the best of Wiesel's art. However, in the context of Wiesel's subsequent fiction, where the narrative strategies are dependent on the interrelation of narrator and listener, or narrator and reader, the simplicity of the mode of narration in *Dawn* marks only the beginning of Wiesel's exploration of fictional techniques. Whereas the narrator in *Dawn* is preoccupied with the moral predicament of the reversal of his role from victim to executioner, the dilemma of the narrators in the novels following *Dawn* is to find ways of telling the tale, using silence as a narrative strategy.

In the opening paragraphs of *Dawn*, the scenic silence is evoked as a prelude to the narrator's story:

> Somewhere a child began to cry. In the house across the way an old woman closed the shutters. It was hot with the heat of an autumn evening in Palestine.
> Standing near the window I looked out at the transparent twilight whose descent made the city seem silent, motionless, unreal, and very far away. Tomorrow, I thought for the hundredth time, I shall kill a man, and I wondered if the crying child and the woman across the way knew.(7)

Within the twelve-hour time span of the novel, stretching from twilight to dawn, the temporal and spatial orientation of the story shifts between the narrator's past to the immediacy of the present. As day changes into night, the narrator recalls an early childhood incident in his home town, when a beggar had taught him how to distinguish day from night: "Always look at a window, and failing that look into the eyes of a man. If you see a face, any face, then you can be sure that night has succeeded day. For believe me, night has a face". The introduction of the beggar in *Dawn* is the beginning of Wiesel's presentation of the timeless figure who embodies Jewish tradition, and who is forever present in Hasidic legend. He appears in various guises in all Wiesel's subsequent novels, culminating in *A Beggar in Jerusalem*, which opens with the vision of a beggar in the traditional disguise of the Messiah, and continues with the beggar as timeless storyteller and messenger, who is able to transmit his tales with both silence and words. As in *A Beggar in Jerusalem*, the beggar appears in *Dawn* as night falls, reminding the narrator that night is purer than day, being more intense and true: "The echo of words that have been spoken during the day takes on a new and deeper meaning". Moreover, the physical description of the beggar hardly changes throughout Wiesel's fiction. As portrayed in *Dawn*, he is "a gaunt, shadowy fellow, dressed in shabby black clothes, with a look in his eyes that was not of this world".

The story itself, which begins in Chapter 1, several pages after the novel opens, is narrated in the style of journalistic reportage. The narrator introduces himself and his story in an abrupt, terse manner:

> Elisha is my name. At the time of this story I was
> eighteen years old. Gad had recruited me for the
> Movement and brought me to Palestine. He had made me
> into a terrorist. (17)

Thereafter, the first person narration of the story gradually builds up to the dramatic action and narrative climax of the novel. Elisha, a survivor of Buchenwald, lives in Paris after the war, studying philosophy at the Sorbonne. one day he is confronted by "a messenger", called Gad[1], who persuades him to join the Jewish resistance movement in Palestine. Elisha accepts and meets Gad three weeks later in Jerusalem where he is told he must kill a man. He has been selected to play the role of executioner to John Dawson, a British army officer who is being held hostage for the threatened execution of David ben Moshe, a resistance fighter. Much of the narration is taken up with the facts of the British occupation in Palestine, the background of the resistance movement and the summaries of news broadcasts made by Ilana, the announcer of The Voice of Freedom. The immediacy of the narration is achieved through the fragments of conversations among various members of the resistance group, as well as through the presentation of brief episodes of terrorist and British activities in the midst of the Israeli Liberation War of 1948.

The dramatic suspense of the novel revolves around the unequivocally stated moral dilemma of the protagonist who is trapped into the untenable position of having to kill a man whom he cannot hate. He realises that the act of killing is so absolute that it involves not only the killer, but "those who have formed him". He feels compelled to share the responsibility for the murder he is about to commit with the ghosts of his past. He summons them into the room at midnight. Among the people who had been part of his childhood is the beggar who "stood head and shoulders above them all". He appeals to the ghosts not to judge him as a murderer.

In vain, he addresses his father, mother, the Rabbi, and other unnamed visitors, but they remain silent. Only the beggar speaks to him, telling him that the young boy who resembles Elisha as a child will answer all his questions. As the representative of Elisha's childhood and of the people inhabiting his past, the boy assures Elisha they are

not judging him:
> Why are we silent? Because silence is not only our dwelling-place but our very being as well. We are silence. And your silence is us. You carry us with you. Occasionally you may see us, but most of the time we are invisible to you. When you see us you imagine that we are sitting in judgement upon you. You are wrong. Your silence is your judge.(73)

The narrative voice embodying Elisha's lost childhood expresses the essence of the silence which pervades his existence as a survivor. The use of the present tense accentuates his immediate predicament which can only be resolved by confronting the silent ghosts of his past. When Elisha suddenly feels the beggar's arm brushing against his, he comes to the realisation that the beggar is not "the Angel of Death but the prophet Elijah". As the beggar looks into Elisha's eyes with an expression that "radiated kindness," Elisha feels his own identity returning and decides to meet John Dawson. The reason he gives Gad for wanting to confront his victim is that it is "cowardly to kill a complete stranger". When he finally introduces himself to John Dawson, he tells him that his name is Elisha, the name of a prophet, who is a disciple of Elijah.

The confrontation with the dead, "the mute heroes" who haunt his imagination in Chapter 4 of the novel, is a narrative device that recurs in all Wiesel's later fiction. In *Dawn* it provides an added dimension to the first-person narrator's account of the events leading to his arrival in Palestine, and particularly to the dusk to dawn vigil before the execution. When he does finally pull the trigger, he comes to the realisation that he has not only killed John Dawson, but: "I've killed Elisha." The ghosts disappear from the room and his comrades who had selected him to play the role of executioner are silent. However, their silence "was different from the silence which all night long had weighed upon mine". Elisha returns to the window, and hearing the sound of the child crying, as "the night lifted," he sees that: "The tattered fragment of darkness had a face. Looking at it, I understood the reason for my fear. The face was my own". Paradoxically, *Dawn* ends with darkness, and not the light of a new day, as the title suggests.

The Accident, the last volume in the trilogy, is usually linked thematically and developmentally with the first two works. It is interesting that the novel's English title, does not attempt to be a translation of its French title, *Le Jour*, possibly because the author's or publisher's decision was not entirely based on thematic considerations. The book, narrated in the first-person, is based on an autobiographical incident when the author, then a United Nations correspondent in New York, met with an accident which left him seriously injured and incapacitated for almost a year. His travel documents as a stateless person could not be renewed which resulted in his becoming an American citizen. Although the background of the story is based on fact, the work is a novel, and prefigures Wiesel's fictional oeuvre. While the seeds are sown for his exploration of narrative techniques in *Dawn*, the roles of the narrator and listener, which become an essential feature of Wiesel's later novels, are manifested for the first time in the narrative structure of *The Accident*.

The first-person narrator, who remains unnamed, is not presented to the reader as the author but as a fictional narrator who is experiencing the events of the story. As the book opens the immediacy of presentation helps to establish the reader's identification with the narrator:

The accident occurred on an evening in July, right in the

heart of New York, as Kathleen and I were crossing the street to go to see the movie *The Brothers Karamazov*.(11)

The narrator then authenticates the exact location of the accident, stating that it happened: "on the corner of Forty-fifth Street, right in front of the Sheraton-Astor". In a similar way, he evokes the passage of time immediately before and after the accident. On a Sunday, after composing a five-hundred word cable for the United Nations "to say nothing," he takes Kathleen to a restaurant in the evening. While waiting at the edge of the sidewalk for "the red light to turn green," the narrator notes that the time shown on the clock in the TWA window is 10.25. The precise details corroborating the time and place of the accident are juxtaposed with the narrator's vague, unspoken thoughts of suicide as he waits for the accident to happen. He imagines himself on a road where he can think of himself without anguish or contempt, "where the dead live in cemeteries and not in the hearts and memories of men". However, his intention of suicide is never overtly expressed. During surgery to save his life, the doctor suspects that his patient had abandoned him and "was on the side of the enemy". But the doctor is never told the circumstances of the accident, and similarly the reader is left in doubt until the last chapter of the book.

Having established the temporal and spatial framework of the story, the narrator then suspends time and space, superimposing the events of the past on the present. While lying in the hospital ward, physically confined in a plaster cast, words that are spoken by Kathleen and the doctor awaken memories of his past life which flood into his consciousness. For this narrator, there is no present without the past: his survival after the accident is a reminder to him of those who did not survive Auschwitz.

The doctor saves a life that the narrator himself does not respect, and Kathleen's love is a love he cannot share except in empty words or deeds. His physical suffering, the sensations of extreme cold followed by a burning fever, are manifestations of past experiences invading his present existence. The shifts of time and place and the change of narrative pace are almost imperceptible as the past merges with the present.

The scenic silence in the novel can be traced from the time of the accident to the gradual enactment of silence in the role of the silent listener. The narrator, regaining consciousness for a traction of a second after the accident, recalls a poem by Dylan Thomas about not going gently into the night, but to "rage, rage against the dying of the light". However, he cannot utter a sound:

> Scream? Deaf-mutes don't scream. They go gently into the night, lightly, timidly. They don't scream against the dying light. They can't: their mouths are full of blood. It's useless to scream when your mouth is filled with blood: people see the blood but cannot hear you scream. That's Why I was silent. And also because I was dreaming of a summer night when my body was frozen. The heat was sickening, the faces bent over me streaming with sweat – sweat falling in rhythmical drops – and yet I was dreaming that I was so cold I was dying. How can one cry out against a dream? How can one scream against the dying of the light, against life that grows cold, against blood flowing out? (19)

The silent scream and the feelings of cold, heat and death recur throughout the book. The narrator's physical pain and discomfort is increased by the simultaneous recollection of past suffering.

Silence accompanies the narrator on his first meeting

with Kathleen, five years previously, as they walk along the banks of the Seine. He asks her not to speak to him as he is still thinking about death: "It is only in silence, leaning over a river in winter, that one can really think about death". He recalls the question he once asked his grandmother: "How should one keep from being cold in a grave in winter?" His grandmother, being a pious and simple woman, who saw God everywhere, "even in evil, even in punishment, even in injustice," replied: "He who doesn't forget God isn't cold in his grave". Later, when Kathleen asks him to talk of himself, he decides to tell her the story of his grandmother. But, he realises it would have to be expressed in words and, "Grandmother could only be expressed in prayers". The narrator is aware that if he reveals his past to Kathleen, who is afraid of silence, she will hate him in the same way as the stranger, a man whom he had met on a voyage to South America, had done.

The encounter with the stranger in *The Accident* is one of Wiesel's most significant and expansive statements in his fiction of the role of the listener in narration. By telling his tale to the nameless and faceless stranger on the ship, the narrator no longer feels the need to throw himself into the sea. He talks to the stranger about death, his mystic dreams, religious passions, memories of concentration camps and his belief that he is a messenger of the dead among the living:

> I talked for hours. He listened, leaning heavily on the
> railing, without interrupting me, without moving,
> without taking his eyes off a shadow that followed the
> ship. From time to time he would light a cigarette and,
> even when I stopped in the middle of a thought or a
> sentence, he said nothing.
> Sometimes I left a sentence unfinished, jumped from one
> episode to another, or described a character in a word

> without mentioning the event with which he was connected. The stranger didn't ask for explanations. At times I spoke very softly, so softly that it was impossible that he heard a word of what I was saying; but he remained motionless and silent. He seemed not to dare exist outside of silence. (50)

When the stranger finally speaks, he says: "I think I'm going to hate you." The narrator's reaction is one of gratitude: "Few people would have had the courage to accompany me lucidly to the end". The role of the listener in this encounter is of one who can listen in absolute silence, hearing words that are not spoken, and respond not with speech but with emotion. In this instance, hatred is the manifestation of listening with understanding. This passage, moreover, is a key to the way Wiesel's narrators tell their tales: with sentences left unfinished, disjointed images and single words used to evoke characters or events.

Later in the novel, the narrator's role is interchanged with the listener's as he remembers an episode in Paris after the war. The memory is evoked by a question Kathleen asks four weeks after the accident: "Who is Sarah?" While still in a coma, the narrator had repeatedly called the name. He tells Kathleen that it was the name of his mother, but "she is dead." He never talks of his mother, thinking to himself: "I loved her but I had never told her". The story-within-a-story of another Sarah, "a girl with blue eyes and golden hair," is narrated in the past tense, yet the fragments of imaginary dialogue between the narrator and his mother paradoxically situate the story in the present.

The narrator had met a girl named Sarah in Montparnasse where she invited him to her room to make love. Not knowing how to refuse her, and feeling awkward and embarrassed, he followed her, without daring to look at her face. When he learned that her name was Sarah, his mother's name, he asked to hear her story:

> There are times when I curse myself. I shouldn't have listened. I should have fled. To listen to a story under such circumstances is to play a part in it, to take sides, to say yes or no, to move one way or the other. From then on there is a before and an after. And even to forget becomes a cowardly acceptance. (95)

Sarah was twelve years old when she was separated from her parents in the concentration camp and sent to a special barracks for the sexual gratification of the camp officers: "Her life had been spared because there are German officers who like little girls her age". She was claimed as a "special" birthday present by "a drunken pig," who "stank of obscenity". The narrator who listens in silence to the story, feels like "screaming like an animal". But he remains silent; his clenched fingers like a vice around his throat:

> Whoever listens to Sarah and doesn't change, whoever enters Sarah's world and doesn't invent new gods and new religions, deserves death and destruction. Sarah alone had the right to decide what is good and what is evil, the right to differentiate what is true from what usurps the appearance of truth.(96)

In the narrative process, the reader's centre of orientation is not focused on the story itself, or on Sarah, the teller of the tale. She only tells the story, the listener creates its meaning. Not only is the tale transformed through the act of listening, but the listener changes through having heard the tale. He calls Sarah a saint, and when she laughs at him, "this laugh which belongs to someone else, to a body without a soul, to a head without eyes", he can no longer listen. He unlocks the door and runs from the house. But he can never forget listening in silence to her story and still curses himself and history, "which has made us what we are: a source of malediction".

The threads of the fragmented stories of the narrator's past, his dialogues with the dead, as well as the immediate conversations in his hospital room, are woven together in the last chapter of the novel. The reader is told that three people come to see him each day: the doctor in the morning, Kathleen in the evening and Gyula in the afternoon: "He alone had guessed. Gyula was my friend". The sudden introduction of this character at the end of the novel, for the purpose of finding a narrative resolution, is an unusual device in Wiesel's fiction. Moreover, the description of Gyula, who is a painter of Hungarian origin and an "excellent storyteller," is unlike Wiesel's enigmatic narrators in his other novels: "Tall, robust, gray and rebellious hair, mocking and burning eyes; he pushed aside everything around him: altars, ideas, mountains". At their first meeting, Gyula provokes the narrator by accusing him of dying: "Aren't you ashamed to be dying?" Gyula then orders him not die before he completes the portrait he intends to paint of him: "Afterwards, I don't give a darn! But not before! Understood?"

The narrator takes pride in their friendship, and "the tough laws" they impose on it as a protection against the "successes and the certainties of the weak":

> True exchanges take place where simple words are called for, where we set out to state the problem of the immortality of the soul in shockingly banal sentences. (118)

The narrator makes several attempts to tell Gyula the story of the accident, but Gyula refuses to listen: "I have no use for your stories!" In his work, Gyula has "found answers to all questions and questions for all answers". He recounts innumerable tales of his adventures and hallucinatory experiences. One day, appearing unusually preoccupied with his work, he asks the narrator to listen, without interruption, to the story of his "unsuccessful drowning." He explains that as he lay on the sand "under the burning, purple sun" after he is rescued, he feels sad and "disappointed at having come back". Only later did the "unsuccessful drowning" make him sing and dance. He is silent for a long while after he tells the story. Gyula's silence is an alternative means of showing the narrator that he does not need to hear the story of his accident to know the truth.

On his last visit to the hospital, Gyula, standing like "a victorious general" at the foot of the narrator's bed, announces that he has finished the portrait: "And now," he says, "you can die". After placing it on a chair, he steps aside:

> My whole past was there, facing me. It was a painting in which black, interspersed with a few red spots, dominated. The sky was a thick black. The sun, a dark grey. My eyes were a beating red, like Soutine's. They belonged to a man who had seen God commit the most unforgivable crime: to kill without a reason. (123)

The artist had discovered the narrator's past and his death wish without being told of it in words. The portrait Gyula had painted of him on canvas expresses the dark silence of the Kingdom of Night with its dense black sky and grey sun. The comparison of his eyes to Chaim Soutine, the expressionist painter, conveys the tormented suffering of the narrator who, like Soutine, was bent on self-destruction. Soutine, in his paintings, had demonstrated the proximity of extreme ugliness and beauty, and as Arnason points out in *A History of Modern Art*, "death and dissolution can involve resurrection". Gyula's portrait too, depicts death and dissolution which can lead to renewal. He has told the story with brush and paint on canvas, showing the futility of language to tell the tale. The viewer, like the listener, must look and listen in silence: "You don't know how to speak; you are yourself only when you are silent". Admonishing him again not to talk, Gyula and the narrator engage in a silent dialogue, in which Gyula is on the side of the living and the narrator defends his right to live with the memory of the dead. The debate is not resolved but in a final gesture to convince the narrator that man's duty is to make suffering "cease, not to increase it" Gyula puts a match to the canvas and waits for it to be reduced to ashes. In the evocative last line of the book, it is left for the reader to decide whether the burning of the canvas destroys the narrator's past or whether the flames of his past will rise up again from the ashes: "He had forgotten to take along the ashes".

The portrait of the narrator is in many ways the culmination of the trilogy and a new beginning for Wiesel's fictional universe. In the narrative process of *The Accident*, Wiesel establishes a variety of narrative strategies for the narrator and listener to tell the tale using silence as an alternative to speech. The first-person narrator is peripherally situated in the succeeding novels, thereby permitting other narrators in various fictional guises, including that of the mute narrator, to tell the tales which cannot be told by words alone.

CHAPTER 3
THE SILENCE THROUGH THE DIALOGUES IN
THE TOWN BEYOND THE WALL

The Town Beyond the Wall is Wiesel's fourth novel but the first fictional work in which the framework of the third-person narrative situation predominates. The departure from the convention of the fictional memoir in his trilogy to the form of the third-person novel allows Wiesel the freedom to explore various narrative strategies that in his subsequent fiction becomes intrinsic to his narrative art. The Olympian narrator, from his vantage point of omniscience, can assume various fictional guises and present varying points of View to expand the reader's awareness and perception during the narration of the story. In this novel it becomes apparent for the first time that Wiesel's literary techniques will determine the way in which his narrators are able to bear witness to a tale that defies being retold. It is only through creating varying levels of silence in the text that the meaning of Wiesel's message is revealed.

In her introduction to *Legacy of Night*, Ellen Fine expresses a view held by most literary critics of Wiesel's fiction:

> His narrative structure is often fragmented: characterised by shifts of point of view, disjointed images, contradictory statements, and a blending of fact and fiction, of history and imagination. The effect produced is similar to the mode of the "Nouveau Roman" and, at the same time, is in keeping with the tradition of the Jewish storyteller who weaves folktales, anecdotes, and parables into the fabric of his texts, transmitting messages that are highly ambiguous. (6)

She maintains that this "peculiar combination of French stylistics and Jewish legends" has caused some critics to view Wiesel's works as collections of short sketches rather than completely developed novels. While these comments on Wiesel's fictional writing can hardly be disputed since fragmentation of the narrative structure does characterise his novels, this aspect should nevertheless be explored as an essential feature within his writing rather than as an evaluative comment about his writing. Although the intention of Fine's study is not to establish whether Wiesel's works are great novels, she believes that "the thrust of his writing does not lie in his literary techniques" because he has openly rejected the notion of art for art's sake. Her view is that Wiesel is "basically a storyteller with something to say," and her approach is centred around "the network of recurring and interlacing themes, leitmotifs and images" appearing in Wiesel's novels. While acknowledging the validity and contribution of this thematic and developmental approach to Wiesel's fiction, it nevertheless does not confront the problems concerned with the way in which he writes, and why there are "shifts of point of view, disjointed images, contradictory statements, and a blending of fact and fiction, of history and imagination." In spite of the creative tension produced by the literary conventions of the modern French novel and the Midrashic genre, "whereby the past is rendered continually present," Wiesel's fiction should be accorded the literary consideration given to novels which are regarded as more conventional. To dismiss his literary techniques because of the uniqueness of his style and the importance of his message is to ignore the multiplicity of perspectives Wiesel conveys through the shifts of point of view of his narrators, which are at the core of his fictional universe.

My approach to *The Town Beyond the Wall* will be focused on the way in which Wiesel structures the novel, how meaning is created and communicated through particular artistic means, and how silence can be traced through the dialogues. In commenting on the norms and procedures of New Criticism of the novel, NW Visser maintains in his article, "An Aspectual Approach to the Novel," that by almost "fetishising" the thematic and moral concerns of the novel, "emphasis on the achieved artistry of literary works" has been scanted: "The result is that the novel is reduced to some or other moral or philosophical position – a code to live by". To deal with literary texts in this manner, he believes, is to risk "trivialising" both the novel and philosophy. But, although the thematic and moral concerns of Wiesel's novels are not in any way trivialised in Fine's *Legacy of Night*, nor can they be underestimated, particularly in the genre of the Literature of Testimony, they should be dealt with in the context of the literary work. The recurring motifs, the Hasidic and Midrashic reverberations and the moral message, should not simply be lifted out of the individual work and be discussed with reference to what he has said elsewhere in his writings. The themes in the novel should be assessed in relation to the point of view of the narrator in a particular temporal and spatial situation. An appraisal of the narrative organisation of the work will reveal the interaction of the narrator with his listener or reader. It is also possible to show that through Wiesel's deliberate fragmentation and constant shifts of point of view, the narrative paradox of the silent narrators becomes evident in the text itself.

The Town Beyond the Wall is structurally divided into four parts: "The First Prayer," "The Second Prayer," "The Third Prayer," and "The Last Prayer," which correspond to the periods of torture the protagonist Michael is forced to endure in prison. This form of torture, named "The Prayers" by an "erudite torturer," is devised to break the prisoner's resistance by keeping him on his feet without moving until he confesses his crime, goes mad or loses consciousness. The torture takes place in a cell called "The Temple," referring no doubt, to the place of worship where Jews pray standing while facing a wall. The novel begins and ends with Michael in prison where he is physically confined in time and space in one cell during three eight-hour periods of interrogation. Every eight hours the prisoner is escorted to the bathroom and on his return finds a different officer on duty. This clearly demarcated period of time corresponds paradoxically to the Aristotelian concept of the unity of time, marked by the 24 hour cycle. However, the duration of his imprisonment during "The Last Prayer," in a cell occupied by three other prisoners, is left open-ended.

Wiesel uses a situation of physical incarceration to free

the imagination of his central narrator Michael from the confines of time and space. Michael's thoughts are allowed to wander back and forth to the near past and the legendary past without having them dwell in the present fictional reality. The narration of the actual experience of the interrogation and torture is kept to a minimum, and the reader is only reminded of it through the desultory conversation of the interrogator with his prisoner. The narrative itself takes place mainly outside the walls of the prison, which not only provides a means for the prisoner to endure his torture, but allows the authorial narrator to make excursions into Michael's past so that the past can be relived as though it were present. In this way, Michael's voice is imprisoned in neither time nor space. The temporal and spatial suspension created through this technique is largely responsible for the fragmentary structure of the novel.

As in Wiesel's other fictional works, the plot of *The Town Beyond the Wall* serves as a framework for the novel, and the reader is required to piece together the disjointed narrative sequences to discover the meaning of the story. The novel opens with a memory of Michael's past, narrated with the immediacy of the present:

> Outside, twilight swooped down on the city like a
> vandal's hand: suddenly, without warning .... No light
> anywhere. Every window blind. The streets almost empty.
> In the square near the Municipal Theatre only old
> Martha, the official town drunk, exuberates. She has the
> whole city to herself, and her performance unfolds in a
> kind of demonic ecstasy. (7)

After recalling her joyous dance and her insulting curses, the narrator's vivid picture of Martha is disturbed by the guard's voice who asks, "What did you say?" As Michael opens his eyes, he replies, "Nothing. I didn't say anything". This pattern of memory interrupted by interrogation occurs throughout the three "Prayers" of the book. The prison officer continually reminds Michael that whether it will take an hour or three days, it is inevitable that as the load in his legs become heavier, he will start screaming and shouting, "begging for the chance to make a long speech." With this form of torture, "it's the legs that turn talkative". But Michael, in spite of his fear of physical pain, knows that he has to remain silent for three days to give his friend Pedro the opportunity to escape.

Michael, a survivor of the concentration camps, lives in Paris after the war in a state of alienation. He wanders aimlessly through the streets, frequenting the world of vagabonds, while trying to understand the events of the past and the meaning to his life. After a chance meeting with a friend of his childhood who assists him to secure a position as a journalist on a Paris weekly, he is assigned to cover a story in Tangiers. It is there that he meets Pedro, "one of those men who cannot be defined in words", with whom he shares the stories of the past which become a link between them. He tells Pedro of his obsessive desire to return to Szerencsevaros in Hungary, the town of his birth and childhood, to try to understand the catastrophe which befell him, his family and the Jewish community. Pedro arranges for his return and accompanies him to the outskirts of the town. They plan to meet after three days to make the journey from behind the Iron Curtain back to Tangiers. As Michael wanders through the streets of the town inhabited by strangers, he suddenly becomes aware of the precise reason for his compulsion to return. At the place where the old synagogue once stood, he remembers a face in the window, who for seven days watched impassively as the Jews were rounded up for deportation. It is this spectator, "neither victim nor executioner," whom Michael wanted to confront. This confrontation leads the spectator to change from his passive role of indifferent observer to informer. As a result Michael is arrested and imprisoned.

The narration of the story alternates between Michael's imprisonment and his present and past experiences in the town to which he returns. The constant references to his legs, which are heavy and wooden throughout his torture, are conveyed not only through the officer's comments but filter through recollections of his youth. As he recalls his adolescent love for Milika, he feels "thousands of mosquitoes jabbing small needles" into his legs. It was Milika who kept the secret of the death of the old man Varady, whose survival had become a legend in the town. As Varady believed implicitly in the mortality of God and the immortality of man, Milika complied with his wish to prolong the legend of his immortality. While this memory triggers off the sensation of immobility in his legs, Michael's confinement is constantly contrasted with his remembrances of his post-Holocaust past, associated with pacing and walking:

> He thought better while he walked; his ideas seemed
> clearer, more dynamic. Later he became Pedro's friend
> for the simple reason that Pedro knew how to walk; few
> people did. Michael came to the conclusion that the legs
> are as useful, as indispensable to the awareness, as the
> eyes or the fingers. No one knows the earth who has not
> walked upon it. (74)

The interaction between Michael and Pedro contained in their dialogues, in the italicised sections of the novel, is the unifying thread in the narrative. Wiesel, in trying out various narrative strategies in this novel, uses the mode of dialogue for the first time as a condensed device of storytelling. This form of narration, which he has subsequently used in *A Jew Today* and *One Generation After*, is not dependent on a temporal or spatial situation. Each dialogue is concerned only with the interrelationship of two people, which conveys an immediacy to the reader that negates the idea of the spatial separation between the speakers. The timelessness of the dialogues in *Town Beyond the Wall*, juxtaposed with the time bound conversations between prisoner and guard, provides the balance in the structural organisation of the novel. The fragments of dialogue, which Wiesel particularly emphasises in italics, not only weave the various strands of the story together but provide the alternative narrative view points of Michael and Pedro who become both the narrators and listeners of the tales.

The pattern of the dialogues is uneven and erratic, appearing frequently in the first section, several times in the second and last part of the novel, and being absent in "The Third Prayer," when the prisoner finally succumbs to a state of unconsciousness. Here the narration of Michael and Pedro's meeting is from the point of view of the omniscient narrator. The length of the dialogues varies from two lines to four pages and their contents are either in the form of an interchange of ideas following the stories Michael or Pedro relate to each other, or are independent exchanges between friends. In the first dialogue, Michael, whose Biblical name means "who is like God," asks Pedro to talk to him about God. Pedro's reply is in the form of an aphorism: "God, little brother, is the weakness of strong men and the strength of weak men." Similarly, his answer to Michael's question about man is: "Man is God's strength. Also his weakness". The subsequent dialogues, however, are on a more personal level. Pedro shares Michael's childhood memories and is able to speak of

Moishe the Madman as though he had known him, "as if the madman were still alive, there, with us". Pedro asks Michael why the madman wept while he sang and laughed when he was silent, and when Michael tells him that Moishe was heartbroken when he sang, Pedro remarks that he likes Moishe's laugh more than his songs. Because Pedro is able to speak of Michael's dead friends, hear their laughter, songs and silences, "he gave them immortality". This shared experience conveyed through the dialogues allows the reader to participate in the stories, which become more meaningful because of the questions, comments and responses of narrator and listener.

Many of Michael's stories about madness provide a link in the narrative chain of the novel. The epigraph of the book, "I have a plan – to go mad," from Dostoyevsky's *The Brothers Karamazov*, is a motif that is followed through from the beginning of the book until Michael's final confrontation with madness in prison. When he is on the verge of madness, each phase of his life is filtered through the dialogues, which provide the continuity of his separate stories. At the age of 13, Michael spends a year with Kalman, a teacher regarded as mad by the community, "who renounces reason at the start in order to find it later, embellished and vigorous, at the heart of madness". Kalman and his three disciples hold themselves outside time: "they were trying to follow Time to its ultimate source". After a while, the other two students plunge into madness, but the Germans "saved" Michael, when "all life as it had been ceased". Pedro questions Michael about the fate of Kalman and his pupils, and Michael's reply is: "They turned into wood. When I saw them for the last time they were on the way to death. The madmen were the first to go". Pedro wonders whether this is the reason for Michael's wish to return to his town, "to see if Kalman left his madness behind, so that you can take it upon yourself". But Michael assures him that it has nothing to do with his teacher and his madness.

During another dialogue Michael tells Pedro he was on the verge of madness when his friend Yankel died. He had spent seven days and seven nights at his bedside trying to talk to him, but Yankel could not hear him. Until that time Michael was never able to forgive Yankel, who was called "the little prince" at the concentration camp at Auschwitz, for being present when Michael was unable to weep as his father lay dying. In spite of Yankel's continual attempts to see Michael in Paris after the war, Michael refuses to speak to him except for one meeting, when he almost vindicates his behaviour to "the little prince," by acknowledging that "sometimes the fount of tears dries up; weeping is also a gift of heaven". But he is unable to transform the memory he believes Yankel has of him. He never sees the boy again until a policeman summons him urgently to the hospital after Yankel's accident. It is then that he tries to justify his own existence and weaves "a universe of hallucinations" blending the past with the future, measuring the destinies of all men with that of his dying friend. He tells Pedro that he might have reached "the kingdom of madness," where there would have been no further torment and anguish but he admits, "The choice of madness is an act of courage." It is also an act of free will that destroys freedom which is only given to man: "God is not free." Pedro applauds the words of Michael and laughs, saying: "I like you, my friend! You're trying to drive God mad. That's why I like you.

In the same way as Michael and Pedro share ideas of madness, so their friendship is sealed and measured by their silences. Michael's literal silence in the novel during his interrogation and imprisonment is actualised in his relationship with Pedro. The silence is contained not only in the act of listening and narrating within the dialogues but is present in the stories, and in the pauses before and after their verbal exchanges. When Michael is about to meet Pedro for the first time in a cafe in Tangiers, he remembers the words of Kalman his teacher:

> Sometimes it happens that we travel for a long time
> without knowing that we have made the long journey
> solely to pronounce a certain word, a certain phrase, in a
> certain place. The meeting of the word is a rare
> accomplishment, on the scale of humanity. (118)

It is at this place, and at this meeting, that Michael finds those certain words to pronounce. He had been listening to tales told in the marketplace by an old storyteller reciting the same tale every night to his audience who showed as much enthusiasm as if they were hearing it for the first time. Michael thinks that "if he were to live another life" he would want to be a teller of tales since the human voice remains the one instrument by which men can share their dreams. When he enters the café he joins a group who are listening to tales of hatred and fear told by a young Muslim, a Romanian sculptor and a shy Spaniard. Suddenly, Michael is asked by a tall, silent stranger to tell them a story. Feeling the power of this man to awaken him to freedom, he searches his memory, "turned pages, weighed episodes, examined faces buried pell-mell in his depths," until he finds the appropriate story. I will quote the story in full to show how Wiesel's literary techniques in the narrative process of the tale achieve his message of silence:

> The hero of my story is neither fear nor hatred: it is
> silence. The silence of a five-year old Jew. His name was
> Mendele. In his eyes the whole sweep of his people's

suffering could be read. He lived in Szerencsevaros, which means in Hungarian the city of luck. One day the Germans decided to rid the country of what they called the Jewish plague. Feige, Mendele's mother, a beautiful and pious young widow, had a visit from an old friend of her husband, a peasant who owned an isolated farm on the other side of the mountain.

'Take your son, Feige, and come with me,' the peasant said to her. 'I owe it to my friend to save his family. Hurry up, now!'

It was night. The streets were deserted. The peasant led the widow and her son to where he had left the wagon. He had them get up into it, and then he said to them: 'I'm going to load the wagon. You'll be buried under the mountain of hay. It has to be done. I'll work out two openings so you can breathe. But be careful! Don't move! Whatever happens, don't budge! And most of all when we leave town, at the sentry station! Tell that to your son, Feige.'

The widow took her son's face in her hands and as she stroked his hair very gently she said to him, 'Did you hear? We must be silent. Whatever happens! It's our only chance. Our lives depend on it. Even if you're afraid, even if you hurt, don't call out, and don't cry! You can scream later, you can cry later. Do you understand, Son?

'Yes, Mother, I understand. Don't worry. I won't cry. I promise.'

At the sentry station two Hungarian gendarmes, black feathers in their hats, asked the peasant where he was going.

'I'm going home,' he answered. 'I have two farms, two fields; the town lies between them. To move hay or wheat from one to the other I've got to cross the city. I've done it so often that the horses know the way themselves.'

What are you hiding underneath?'
'Nothing officers. Nothing at all I swear it. I have nothing to hide.'
The gendarmes drew their long swords from their black scabbards and drove them into the hay from all angles. It went on forever. Finally the peasant couldn't stand it any longer; he let out a whimper, and tried to smother it with the back of his hand. Too late. One of the gendarmes had noticed. The peasant had to unload the hay; and the gendarmes, triumphant saw the widow and her son.
'Mama,' Mendele wept, 'it wasn't me who called out. It wasn't me'.
The gendarmes ordered him off the wagon, but he couldn't move. His body was run through. 'Mama,' he said again, while bloody tears ran into his mouth, 'it wasn't me, it wasn't me' The widow, a crown of hay about her head, did not answer. Dead. She too had kept silence. (119-120)

When Michael completes his tale a thick silence falls on the group as the party breaks up, leaving Michael and the tall man face to face. It is not only the theme and the characters of the story that portray silence; it is conveyed as well through the narrator's choice of words and phrases, the brevity of his sentences, the pauses after each dialogue, and the staccato rhythm of the narration.

Mendele's silence is the link between Michael and Pedro: "It is the silence that sets off our steps" when they are alone or "with someone who moves us, with someone who leans towards us". As they walk in silence side by side, Michael discovers the texture, the depth and the music of silence. He realises that he is no longer alone, that "silence was not an emptiness but a presence." He talks to Pedro of his childhood, "as if he were compelled to transfuse to his friend the images and dreams of his past". Puffing at his pipe, Pedro listens, his sensitive face changing constantly, displaying horror, surprise, recognition, anger, "most of all pride." Everything he hears brings about a change in his eyes which either darken, deepen or burn brighter: "Only mystics are capable of listening with such intensity". It is through the transmission of his tales and Pedro's response of laughter, sadness or silence that Michael is able to understand the full meaning of his own past. The acts of narrating and listening become a sacred link between them, culminating in Pedro's words to Michael: "From now on you can say 'I am Pedro,' and I, 'I am Michael.'" This exchange of identity leads to the reversal of roles between narrator and listener, crucial to the resolution of the novel through its narrative process.

In "The Last Prayer" there is an almost imperceptible change in the dialogues and in the mode of narration, which shifts from the third-person narrative situation to first-person narration. After Michael regains consciousness in a prison cell, having survived the torture of the three "prayers," he finds himself together with a madman, a mute boy and Menachem, a handsome Jew, "with the moving face of a Byzantine Christ." He is only able to converse briefly with Menachem, who although touched with madness, possesses his own "poetic coherence." But Michael imagines Pedro in the cell, and the dialogues between them continue with more frequency, urgency and immediacy than elsewhere in the novel:

"Listen to me, Pedro. Listen."

"I'm listening," he said with an intelligent smile.

"I have to tell you what happened, I have to."

"Go on."(148)

Michael notices a change in Pedro, which alerts the reader to his new role as absent listener. Although Pedro tilts his head to the right, as he always does when he is listening, he is not smoking his pipe, and "Pedro without his pipe seems different: armless." Michael asks him again whether he is listening, and only when he feels reassured that there is a listener to hear his tale, does he begin, in the first-person, the narration of his return to Szerencsevaros. As he walks through the town filled with strangers, they re-awaken memories of his mother, his father and the apostate Gabriel who returned unwanted to the town to share the fate of the community. The narrative suspense of his story, and the climax of the novel itself, comes about when Michael suddenly realises "the real" reason for his return – the violent memory of the face in the window. But again his dialogue with Pedro fragments the story as he asks him whether he is listening and is able to understand. The burning question that torments him, and he needs to transmit, is: "How a human being can remain indifferent". He is able to understand the executioners and the victims but not the spectator who watched the cruelty of the Hungarian police behind the curtains of a window for seven days as the great courtyard of the synagogue filled and emptied:

> The spectator is entirely beyond us. He sees without
> being seen. He is there but unnoticed. The footlights hide
> him. He never applauds nor hisses; his presence is
> evasive, and commits him less than his absence might.
> He says neither yes nor no, and not even maybe. He says
> nothing. He is there but he acts as if he were not. Worse:
> he acts as if the rest of us were not. (161-162)

As the narrative pace of the novel quickens while Michael prepares to confront the spectator, Wiesel inserts four repetitive phrases in italics, before Michael reveals the purpose of his visit: "'I'm thirsty,' my little sister said".

This silent indictment of the spectator through Michael's vivid memory of his eight-year old sister is more powerful than his attempt to humiliate the anonymous observer with verbal abuse. Michael discovers through his conversation with him that the man regarded himself as a spectator in a game others were playing, "you on one side, the Germans and the police on the other." He feels no shame, no remorse and no sadness, nor is he prepared to be humiliated by his accuser. Ignoring his continual protests to be humiliated, Michael says:

> The dead Jews, women gone mad, the mute children –
> I'm their messenger. And I tell you they haven't forgotten
> you. Someday they'll come marching, trampling you,
> spitting in your face. And at their shouts of contempt
> you'll pray God to deafen you. (172)

The only emotion the spectator displays is his need for Michael to hate him: "Your contempt would burn at my eyes; they'd never close again! You've got to hate me!". But Michael rejects hatred as an inadequate response, and because of this, the spectator has him arrested. Anticipating his victory, the spectator says, "Now you'll have to hate me."

The dialogue following Michael's narration of the story is characteristic of the imaginary response of his listener:

> "Did you spit in his face?" Pedro asked.
> "No."
> "The man turned you in, and you didn't spit in his face?"
> "No, my friend. I smiled at him. I smiled at the man to whom I had played God."
> And he rubbed his forehead, absorbed; he always did that when he was moved. (174-175)

In *Legacy of Night*, Ellen Fine expresses the opinion that

Michael's confrontation with the indifferent bystander demonstrates how "the spoken word liberates him from his internal prison and brings him closer to a reconciliation with the past". However, in the way in which the novel is structured, and particularly through the dialogues, it is Michael's silence and not his words that liberates and reconciles him with his past. The intimacy of his relationship with Pedro is built on silence and unanswered questions. The stories about madness, as well as the laughter and suffering they share, are alternative responses to speech in Wiesel's fictional universe. The essence of Michael's existence is contained in one of his dialogues with Pedro, while discussing the death of a child: "It's when I'm silent that I live; in silence I define myself". While the confrontation with the spectator is important for the narrative resolution and the thematic concerns of the novel, it nevertheless is confined to the story Michael narrates to his absent friend, and must be viewed in the context of the narrative organisation of the book as a whole.

Towards the end of the novel the omniscient narrator resumes the narration of Michael's imprisonment: "Days and nights flowed by in the gloom that swallowed them up one after another". Michael tries to recall Pedro and resume their dialogue, but he feels that his friend, now in Spain, is too far away, "cloaked in fog and forgetfulness", and is not listening to him. It is only when Michael saves the mute boy, "the Silent One," from being throttled by the madman in their cell that Pedro "came to visit," significantly again without his pipe. In their last dialogue he tells Michael that he is proud of him for saving a human life. In spite of Michael's explanation that he only saved a body "with a sleeping mind and a dead soul," Pedro smiles as if remembering something:

> "You're smiling Pedro, and I'm going mad. I have no strength left. I'm at the end of the line. I can't do any more. I'm alone. To stay sane I've got to have someone across from me. Otherwise my mind will rot, and smell of decay, and twist like the serpent that feels the earth and death." Pedro went on smiling: "That's exactly what I want you to do: recreate the universe. Restore that boy's sanity. Cure him. He'll save you." (182)

After the dialogue, Michael's strength flows back as he welcomes the new dawn. He is suddenly responsible for a life and "would resume the creation of the world from the void". Michael, in trying to establish a rapport with the mute boy, feeds him from his own rations. As soon as he feels confident that there is a response from him, he shows him how to dance, sing, laugh and weep: "he had to show the boy that being a man meant all this". And he tells him endless stories – sad tales, funny adventures, "even obscene stories." The boy however, remains silent and indifferent. Although Michael thinks his efforts have been futile, he nevertheless, says:

> One day the ice will break and you'll begin to smile: for me that will be proof of our strength, of our compact. Then you'll shake yourself and the shadows will fall away from you as the fever leaves a sick man: you'll open your eyes and you'll say to yourself, 'I feel better, the sickness is gone, I'm different.' You'll tell me your name and you'll ask me, 'Who are you?' and I'll answer, 'I'm Pedro'. And that will be a proof that man survives, that he passes himself along. Later in another prison, someone will ask your name and you'll say, 'I'm Michael.' And then you will know the taste of the most genuine of victories. (188-189)

This monologue within the silent dialogue contains the

essence of Wiesel's narrative strategies in *The Town Beyond the Wall*. Only when there is a narrator and a listener, and their roles can be interchanged, can the continuity of the stories be maintained. When Michael can say, 'I'm Pedro', and Pedro can say 'I'm Michael,' storytelling becomes an inviolable link between them. Whether Pedro is a silent presence or an imagined absence in their dialogues, Michael is able to transmit his stories. Providing there is a listener, even if he is mute, the tale can be told in order for it to be retold when the listener assumes his new role as narrator. The last sentence of the book reveals the identity of "the Silent One": "The other bore the Biblical name of Eliezer, which means 'God has granted my prayer.'" While the conclusion offers no resolution to the novel, which from the outset defies logical ordering, it does nevertheless suggest to the reader that Eliezer has heard the tale, and having heard it, will be the silent link in the chain of storytelling.

CHAPTER 4
SILENCE AS A NARRATIVE PRESENCE IN
THE GATES OF THE FOREST

Of all Wiesel's fictional works, *The Gates of the Forest* is perhaps his most complex and challenging. In this work the profundity of silence, which is the author's central response to the Holocaust, is evoked not only through the dramatisation of silence as a theme but is embedded functionally in the narrative process. Wiesel evokes and mobilises silence through his narrators in ways that expand its meaning beyond the limitations of language and the boundaries of storytelling. Because silence is a justifiable alternative to the verbal transmission of the tale, the reader bears the burden of incorporating that silence into the text as an integral part of the reading experience. Often, the absence of words or the pauses in the narration, the unfinished stories or the broken dialogues that constantly shift between present and past, provide the narrative means of transmitting the tale of Jewish survival after Auschwitz. The reader must be made aware of the value attached to the absence of words, since the balance between language and silence shapes and textures the meaning of the novel.

Part of the complexity of *The Gates of the Forest* lies in the multiple perspectives it offers. As the title suggests, there are gates that lead into and out of the forest. At times, the gates are only partially opened by the narrators' stories to allow the reader glimpses into the labyrinth of pathways leading everywhere and nowhere. There are gates through which the narrators can go back through time and retrace their steps through the *shtetls* of their childhood, or go forward into a void in which Jewish life no longer exists. Some gates lead into the solitude and silence of the forest, while others are passageways into a post-Holocaust world of madness. One gate initiates the way to absurd laughter, and another is an entrance to speechlessness. Each gate provides a different focus on and perception of survival, both in and out of the forest. The gates are also representations of unanswerable questions, always remaining open and vulnerable. The constant movements back and forth on paths that are familiar in terms of past journeys, or are unknowable in relation to the present upheaval and future uncertainty, allow infinite possibilities of interpretation in this novel. There are continual beginnings and reversals in the stories from which the reader should neither expect conclusions nor anticipate solutions.

The process of reversal is paradoxically presented in the structural organisation of the book which is divided into four parts, corresponding to the seasonal cycle of the year – Spring, Summer, Autumn and Winter. The process of rebirth and recreation suggested by this division reinforces the discordance of existence rather than emphasises the natural rhythmic cycle of nature. In the Spring, the protagonist survives the war by hiding in a dark cave of a forest in Transylvania, under the assumed name of Gregor. He has pledged an oath of silence to his father who had brought him to the forest, promising never to reveal his real name until after the war.

After his meeting with a stranger in the forest, who saves and then changes his life, Gregor moves out of the forest. In the section "Summer," he takes refuge in the Christian world by posing as a deaf mute. In the third part of the novel, "Autumn," Gregor returns to another forest with a group of Jewish partisans to whom he brings the message of the destruction of the European Jewish communities. The last section of the book, "Winter," ironically begins with a Hasidic celebration in New York where Gregor finally confronts the burden of his past. The change of seasons that demarcates four different episodes in Gregor's life is in fact only a framework for the organisation of the novel. Within each season the rhythmic pattern is disturbed by unnatural events so that the growth and development of the protagonist is stunted and ruptured by frequent journeys into the past from which he cannot extricate himself. When Gregor is in the forest in the first and third parts of the novel, his imagination and the stranger's haunting presence lead him out of the forest into the world of his Hasidic childhood; when he is out of the forest, his memories and his irrevocable ties with the stranger, draw him back to the solitude and security of the forest. If there is a correspondence between the seasons and Gregor's life, then it is "Winter" and not "Spring" that suggests continuance.

In offering an explanation of how the four parts of the

novel can be understood in relation to four motifs from Jewish history, Tedd Estess maintains in Elie Wiesel:
> The first part, "Spring" echoes the experience of chaos and creation in Genesis; "Summer" corresponds especially to the experience of anti-Semitism in the Christian West; "Autumn" recalls the action of the Jewish rebels through the centuries; "Winter" emphasises religious community and family solidarity as responses to loneliness in human life.(66)

While Estess is not suggesting that Wiesel consciously organised his story with these motifs in mind, he maintains that all Wiesel's narratives reach beyond themselves into the long history of Jewish experience often by reversing elements of Jewish tradition.

Since Biblical times, the number "four" has been a sacred and mystical number for Jews, and it is interesting to note that the four parts of the novel are complemented by the four chapter divisions in "Spring," "Autumn" and "Winter." In the first section of the novel, which contains the essence of the narrative, the four chapters correspond to the four fictional works preceding *The Gates of the Forest*. The scene of the first chapter is set on a moonless night in the forest, recalling Wiesel's first book *Night*, in which the narrator loses his innocence, his father and his faith in the dark regions of the "Kingdom of Night." Chapter 2 begins with the breaking of dawn, the title of his second novel, where between twilight and dawn, the son of a victim changes his role to executioner. The third chapter opens with the morning of a new day, re-echoing the French title, of his third work, *Le Jour*, which examines the dilemma of the protagonist facing a choice between life and death in a post-Holocaust world. The opening lines of the fourth chapter: "Slowly and monotonously the days went by," correspond to the slow and monotonous days of Michael's endurance in a prison cell in *The Town Beyond the Wall*. These analogies seem to suggest that Wiesel is working within the boundaries of the Aristotelian unity of time and yet by reversing the order of day and night, as well as the seasons of the year, he is creating a disruption of the conventional time scheme.

Just as the paradoxical structuring of the novel adds a further dimension to its meaning, so the narrative process is complicated by the interchangeability of the roles and identities of the narrators. The opening two paragraphs of the book are the key to the identity of the nameless narrator who dominates the first part of the narrative by his laughter and thereafter by his absence.

> He had no name, so he gave him his own. As a loan, as a gift, what did it matter? In time of war every word is as good as the next. A man possesses only what he gives away.
>
> Gregor loved and hated his laugh, which was like no other, which did not even resemble itself. (13) [1]

The giving away of a name is significant in several ways in this novel. According to Jewish tradition, names are an embodiment of man's identity and traditional roots. On the death of a parent or grandparent, the name is given to the child to perpetuate his or her memory and ensure continuity in the family. The supreme importance of names in a pre-Holocaust world is contrasted with its loss of meaning after Auschwitz, when language becomes distorted and words undergo a process of inversion.

In *The Gates of the Forest* both narrators lose their names for different reasons. The real name of the young protagonist, who calls himself Gregor, "has gone into hiding", typifying thousands of Jews who lived under false names and identities during the war. Realising that the laws of normal life are no longer valid, Gregor feels that he has the right to give away his name and considers himself "lucky" to present the name of his "father's father" to the nameless stranger. When Gregor reveals his Biblical name Gavriel, which is that of an angel, and means "man of God," the stranger assures him that he will not disclose it: "I can keep silent. That's what I do best. I can keep my mouth shut, even under torture. Or open my mouth and say nothing". Gregor gives away his name just before dawn, while it is still dark, having not yet seen the face of the stranger. He has only heard his soft "curious" voice, his laughter and his fearful silence. The way in which the name is received in the silence of the forest prefigures Gavriel's simultaneous presence and absence in the narrative and establishes the inexorable link between the two men who share a name and identity. The loss of Gavriel's original name is presented in an ambiguous way, creating a strange sense of invisibility around the nameless stranger. His real name is never disclosed to the reader, and his ironic comments to Gregor that his name is dead and "went away one day" are offered as though a name has a fate of its own: "Sometimes a name ages, falls ill, and dies much before the man who bears it". And yet, when he tells Gregor that he has come from the town at the foot of the mountain, "empty of Jews" but "crowded with ghosts" and "names without bodies," he says that the Germans have been able to kill the Jews but "they can't find a way of erasing their names". In spite of the stranger's belief that "every name has something immortal and eternal about it which defies time," and is thus indestructible, the death of his own name seems to contradict the idea of continuity. The burden of his own survival as a messenger from the dead to the living does not allow him to recover his name and pass it on as an act of faith for future generations.

In the opening pages of the novel, Wiesel uses the scenic silence of the forest as an accompaniment to the strange encounter between Gregor and Gavriel. Moments before their meeting on a moonless night, as Gregor is about to fall asleep, he hears an unfamiliar sound and feels an imperceptible presence, which he immediately presumes is coming from the clouds. He looks up and listens, but the clouds "were making no sound, at least not yet". The image of the soundless clouds is a scenic dimension of the silence of the Holocaust which foreshadows Gregor's realisation that the clouds are not natural phenomena but are "Jews driven from their homes and transformed into clouds". He calls out: "Who's there?" There is no answer: "Silence. Nothing. Night, clouds, the forest". The silence functions not only as a narrative device of suspense, heightening Gregor's solitude in the darkness of the forest, but becomes an essential constituent of the dialogue between the strangers when they exchange names, roles and stories.

Before Gregor sees the stranger, he hears his laughter and shudders with fear: "Behind every tree and within every shred of cloud someone was laughing." It was not the ordinary laughter of one man but "of a hundred, of seven times seven hundreds". Gregor begs the man to stop laughing and shouts to him in German: "Listen to the war and you won't laugh any longer." After a lengthy silence as the clouds become thicker, a voice speaking in Yiddish answers: "I'm listening to the war and I'm laughing." The stranger, believing he is the last survivor, thinks he has every right to laugh, because "to weep is to play their game". His laughter is at times sad, passionate or mad; he neither laughs with cruelty nor joy, but as a man who has known total fear and is no longer afraid of anyone or anything. When he laughs without uttering a word, Gregor understands that "the event was so heavy with horror, experienced or anticipated, that words could not really contain it". Gavriel's absurd laughter echoes through the cave and into the forest, and, long after he disappears, it continues to reverberate throughout the book whenever his name or voice is evoked. His laughter is an alternative narrative device of speech and a constant reminder of Gavriel's haunting presence, even in his absence. In his article "Silence and Laughter," Arthur A. Cohen describes some aspects of this laughter:

> There is one counterfoil to silence in Wiesel's fiction. When silence dries up speech and can no longer be textured, when the legends have been told and the stories unravelled, when the silence of Wiesel's characters can do no more, they do something even more incredible than shut their mouths: they laugh. The obsessional laugh, known to me only in Leonid Andreyev's grotesque story *The Red Laugh*, is the only reply. And to whom does the laughter go forth? Whom else but to God. The tormentors never laugh. Wiesel does not allow the persecutors to laugh. They are permitted everything but silence and laughter. These are the weapons, the only weapons which deserted heroes and forsaken martyrs can shoulder: to be silent and to break their souls in laughter. (37)

As in most of Wiesel's fiction, the reader is given very little insight into the characters of the narrators. The scanty descriptions of their physical characteristics often serve to emphasise their elusive and shadowy existence. Gavriel is described as having "a thousand names" and "a thousand voices," yet his eyes distinguish him from other men: they are "two firebrands which sear the flesh and pierce the skin of being. They gaze upon you; you will never be the same". No description is offered of Gregor, however, except that at the time of his encounter with Gavriel, his age is given as 17. It is only in the exchange of stories of their past, as well as through their dialogues, that Gregor and Gavriel assume separate, though interchangeable, identities. When Gregor tells Gavriel stories about his father, Gavriel responds as though he had known him and tells Gregor: "I like that father of yours". Furthermore, the imaginative dialogue Gregor has with his grandfather, who had died ten years previously, is an acknowledgement of the reason for Gavriel's presence in the forest. He tells his grandfather that he had met a madman "who had lost all ties to man and the meaning of words." His grandfather, with a smile, replies:

> Are you so sure he was mad? Perhaps he was a messenger looking for a message, and for that reason he had neither home nor name; he was one of those dreamers, who wander on the mountainside or roads the world over, who have chosen exile in order to detach themselves from time and exorcise it. Are you sure, my child, that he was mad? (22)

Significantly, Gregor relates his stories by day while Gavriel recounts his stories only when night falls. Gavriel's tales moreover, are always characterised by interruptions of silence and laughter.

One story, Gavriel begins hesitantly, as though he is reluctant to tell it, is the story of Moshe the Mute, who became his friend, after they cut out his tongue. This tale, divulged gradually in incomplete fragments by the omniscient narrator, not only explains the strange friendship between Gavriel and Moshe, but is the key to the binding relationship and interdependence of the two narrators who share a name. Gavriel had reason to believe that Moshe the Mute, who suddenly appeared one day in his community and became the beadle in the synagogue, was "the one for whom the world was waiting, as the earth waits for rain". In spite of Gavriel's constant reproaches and pleas for his intervention as the ghettos were decimated and "the streams ran with blood", the beadle remained intransigent. Soon, Gavriel discovered that Moshe, having acquired wealth and respectability in the community, no longer spent his nights in prayer and weeping. Gavriel believed then that Moshe had waited too long and, "instead of saving men he had let them contaminate and corrupt him." His fall involved the fall of all generations to come: "The Messiah came and nothing changed," and "the executioner goes right on executing". Even when the fatal day came and the Jews were rounded up and led to the forest to be executed, the former beadle "looked on and did nothing." It was only after one of the killers cut out his tongue that he became a beadle again, but it was too late: "He took with him his silence, his secret, his shadow". After the tale is told, Gavriel tells Gregor, with the same laugh he had uttered when he first appeared in the forest, that he thinks of Moshe constantly:

> I think of nothing else. That's the way we're made, I
> guess, to be blinded by presence and haunted by absence.
> I think of him all the time, and I laugh. Tomorrow you'll
> laugh when you think of me. (58)

After hearing the story, which Gavriel urges him to retell, "a dozen times, more if necessary", until he understands its full meaning, Gregor becomes part of the tale by sharing its message of silence. From this point in the narrative, Gregor, too, becomes blinded by Gavriel's presence and haunted by his absence, which is precipitated by Gavriel's surrender to the approaching Hungarian police to save Gregor's life. Before leaving his friend in the forest, Gavriel offers him "the secret key to a secret door": "You must learn to listen. Listening gives you a key. You know that the man was my friend, but you don't realise that he's yours as well". This lesson transforms Gregor's behaviour when he leaves the forest and establishes the act of listening as an analogue to the narration of each story in the novel.

As the heavy silence invades the forest, Gregor believes that "the last of the gates is closed". The silence can be seen in "the eyes of the dogs," and has "the smell of torture," "the odour of a prisoner who has been jeered and beaten and left to die". The silence has penetrated the visual and sensory perceptions of the narrator, giving it an added dimension. In the last words Gavriel utters, he opens yet another door for Gregor, revealing the meaning of their encounter and their parting:

> I'd like you to know only this: separation contains as
> much of a mystery as meeting. In both cases a door
> opens: in meeting it opens on the future, in separation on
> the past. It's the same door. (59)

On leaving his friend in the cave, Gavriel strides down the hill. As he confronts the soldiers and the barking dogs, "he burst suddenly into overwhelming laughter", a sound that resonates in the memory of the reader throughout the ensuing narrative.

With the apparent disappearance of Gavriel from the story, the second part of the book, "Summer," becomes less complex from a narrative point of view, and is dominated by the dramatic action of Gregor's role as a deaf mute. After leaving the forest Gregor finds his way to the village where his family's former servant, Maria, lives. His father had described the exact location of the village and Maria's house to him before securing his safety in the forest. Maria, determined to keep Gregor with her until after the war, devises a plan that will not arouse the suspicion of the villagers. She gives him a new identity, a past and a story; he becomes her "deaf and dumb nephew, slow-witted, harmless, a little odd", the son of her beautiful, but wayward sister, Ileana, whom all the men of the village desired. Maria, repeating Gavriel's advice to Gregor, admonishes him to listen without answering, "and if possible, without understanding":

> And so, by the grace and will of Maria, Gregor gave up speech. This was no sacrifice at all. Already in the cave he had become used to silence and loved it. Gavriel had told him: 'Men talk because they're afraid, they're trying to convince themselves that they're still alive. It's in the silence after the storm that God reveals himself to man. God is silence.' (71)

Within a short time Gregor comes to know the village characters and becomes the best informed person in the community. He hears stories of their joys and sorrows, their forbidden dreams and their hidden love for his "mother." He becomes the receptacle for their inhibitions, guilts and anxieties because: "He knew how to listen; he knew nothing else". Gregor is able to keep his silence not only because his survival depends on it, as it did in the forest, but because the voice of Gavriel "vibrated within him, regulating his breathing and giving depth to his silence".

Gregor is finally forced to break his silence after he is coaxed by the school teacher, Constantine Stefan, to play the part of Judas Iscariot in the school play. When he appears in the third act, the actors and audience react violently, shouting abuse, spitting on him and beating him with their fists, demanding that he repent for betraying and murdering Christ: "Convulsed, the crowd was delirious with an ancient hate, suddenly reawakened". At that moment, Gregor sees a face in the crowd who silently, without words, asks him whether he needs his help. As their eyes meet "a deep and imperishable bond was created between them", and when Gregor finally breaks his pledge of silence, the words he speaks are directed to the stranger Petruskanu to whom he reveals his name and identity:

> This confession will be my last. That I am not Judas you already know. And I have told you that I am not Deana's son, either. All I have left to tell you is this: my name is not Gregor. I am a Jew and my name is a Jewish name, Gavriel. (118)

As "the executioners" move towards the stage "to avenge their honour in blood," Gregor's eyes again meet those of Petruskanu to bid him a silent farewell. But the enigmatic stranger, who curiously reminds the reader of Gavriel, comes dramatically to the rescue and conveys Gregor in his carriage to a place of safety. The brief scene of their encounter is told with the minimum amount of words. Petruskanu tells Gregor he will take him to the partisans the following day; his tone of voice did not call for an answer. Gregor wants to talk to him about Gavriel but he remains silent, thinking he would do so at their next meeting. The knowledge they share is that Petruskanu had known Ileana, but Petruskanu saves Gregor not only for her sake: "I liked seeing you face the crowd, face pain and injustice impassively, contemptuous of everything that could have destroyed you" Although Petruskanu is not mentioned again in the novel, his words, his silence and his sudden disappearance from the story, establish a link between him, Gavriel and Gregor. Moreover, Petruskana provides a key to the gate leading back to the forest where Gregor meets the Jewish partisans and renews his quest for Gavriel.

"Autumn" in the forest has a narrative dimension different from the first part of *The Gates of the Forest*. The scenic silence is still an accompaniment to Jewish survival in a world gone mad, and, at first, the forest retains the propensity to listen and remember: "nothing that is said in its midst is lost". But, for Gregor, the narrator, speech replaces silence as he bears Gavriel's message of the annihilation of the Jewish communities to the fearless leader of the partisans, Leib the Lion. His meeting with Leib, a childhood friend from the ghetto, is portrayed in direct contrast to his encounter with Gavriel whose presence he still feels in the wind, among the leaves, the night and the silence of the forest. Although Gregor and Leib share memories of their youth, Leib cannot comprehend Gregor's silences, needing constant reassurances with words that the stories he hears are based on facts and not madness. At first, Leib refuses to acknowledge the evidence that Gavriel had transmitted to Gregor: "that the earth and sky of Europe had become great, haunted cemeteries". Furthermore, Gregor repeats Gavriel's words to Leib that: "the Messiah is not coming; he got lost along the way, and from now on the clouds will obscure his sight". Incredulous that Gregor feels the urgency to find and rescue Gavriel after he had been captured, Leib surmises that if Gavriel ever existed, he would, since then, have been deported or killed by the enemy. The reply Gregor offers in defence of Gavriel's existence reinforces the reader's conviction that Gavriel's voice, though heard through the imagination of Gregor, is the predominant voice in the novel: "Sometimes I doubt the existence of Gregor, but never that of Gavriel". Having taken over

Gavriel's role as messenger from the dead, Gregor becomes the narrator of Gavriel's tales. Thus, Gavriel's absence from the story serves as both an eloquent and silent presence in the narrative process. But, ironically, the doubts cast by Leib and his friends on Gavriel's existence are more convincing than the subsequent story Wiesel weaves of Leib's plan to find Gavriel.

Once Leib takes control, he, and not Gregor, "reports" the story of the massacre of the Jews to the partisans. He announces his decision to launch "Operation Gavriel," finally convinced that it is an obligation: "To save the only Jew who has information about the fate of our brothers". Leib's plan involves his girlfriend Clara and Gregor, who must go into the town, pretending to be lovers, to gain information about Gavriel from the prison guard. After three days, Leib plans to meet them in the main square of the town to assess the situation. Gregor and Clara find that they are able to converse easily with Janos the guard, whom they convince through Clara's invention of an elaborate story, of their need to find a particular Jew whom they believe is in the prison. The description Gregor gives of him is that he is tall and thin, has a black beard, feverish eyes, and: "He always laughs a lot". On the day they arrange to meet Leib, who does not appear at the prearranged time or place, Janos gives Gregor the news that the Jew is in prison, is being interrogated and tortured and will be deported the following day. However, Janos says he is puzzled by the description Gregor had given him, as the prisoner who was captured on that very day, has no beard, is fair, and does not laugh. Their futile search for Gavriel has led to Leib's capture.

The gate by which Gregor re-enters the forest to bring the message of Leib's fate to the partisans is through speech. He is no longer permitted the alternative of silence as a mode of communication and is obliged to speak in his own voice to explain Leib's disappearance. As he assumes the burden of guilt for his complicity for Leib's imprisonment, he is compelled to repeat every detail of the story four times to his suspicious and grieving audience. Each time he completes the story he is asked to begin again in the hope that there will be a different ending. Gregor knows that "the repetition of the truth betrays it", and the more he talks the more he empties himself of truth. When he tells the story for the fourth time, adding and omitting nothing, repeating every word his listeners have already heard three times before, he changes his voice, as Gavriel used to do, and the story sounds new: "They listened as if they were hearing it for the first time". But then their questions begin, and Gregor "by his words" pushes himself "to the uttermost limits of evil". In desperation, he confesses that he betrayed his friend Leib the Lion to Janos. By continually repeating his betrayal and guilt, Gregor realises that "To live is to betray the dead".

Wiesel, through using different narrative strategies to tell a similar story, is showing how language distorts what ultimately can only be conveyed by silence. Gregor's first encounter in the forest with Gavriel is realised through the narration of stories punctuated by silence and laughter, while his second encounter with Leib and the partisans is portrayed by repetitive language, an inadequate and destructive response to evil. Whereas Gavriel's presence in the first part of the novel enhances the silence of the forest, Leib and the partisans break the spell of silence in the forest in the "Autumn," by expressing events through words. The contrast between the two encounters is marked not only by the presence and absence of the narrative voice of Gavriel, the alternative narrator in the novel, but through the act of listening. only when the listener can receive the unspoken words in the narrator's tale and retell it with words pervaded by silence can the truth of the reality be revealed.

Gregor's quest for Gavriel continues in the fourth and final section of the novel. His meeting with the Hasidic community and their Rabbi opens a gate for him to religion through the fervour of dance, song and prayer. It is a gate of Hasidic faith and ecstasy that his grandfather had opened to him in his childhood. But Gregor, wrapped in years of silence and solitude, is reluctant to enter. He is unable to comprehend how the Rabbi can still believe in God after Auschwitz and behave as though nothing had changed: "To you everything seems simple and this simplicity hurts me". He would prefer the Rabbi to raise his arms to heaven and cry out, "No, I'll have no morel I won't accept it!" But the Rabbi, weighing every word and pausing after every sentence, explains to Gregor that prayer and compassion are more powerful weapons than outcries of anger:

> When you come to our celebrations you'll see how we dance and sing and rejoice. There is joy as well as fury in the hasid's dancing. It's his way of proclaiming. 'You don't want me to dance; too bad, I'll dance anyhow. You've taken away every reason for singing, but I shall sing. I shall sing of the deceit that walks by day and the truth that walks by night, yes, and of the silence of the dusks as well. You didn't expect my joy, but here it is; yes, my joy will rise up; it will submerge you. (196)

Gregor's dispute with the Rabbi when he first meets him, recalls the Biblical story of Jacob's life-and-death struggle with the angel presented in the opening page of the novel, when Gregor is in the forest. Gregor imagines that if the angel of love and the angel of wrath were both victorious, the laughter would "rise above their corpses as if to say, your death has given me birth; I am the soul of your conflict, its fulfilment as well". According to the Rabbi's interpretation of the story, Jacob was victorious and allowed the angel to go free. In showing his gratitude, the angel brought Jacob a ladder on which to build a future. The Rabbi asks Gregor to bring him this ladder, thus offering him a way to transform his suffering into hope, his silence into song and prayer. But when Gregor asks which of them is Jacob, the Rabbi can only answer: "I don't know. Do you?". He intimates that if Gregor has followed the wrong path, he must turn back and "knock at another door", extracting a promise from him to return to the Synagogue and attend their celebration.

The scene Gregor witnesses when he returns to the Hasidic celebration is one of joy and ecstasy as the hasidim climb invisible ladders, and sing the music of the songs without words because "the soul has no need of words". Gregor is tempted "to taste joy, to declare that it's man's ally and not his mirage", yet he remains alone and silent in the crowd. Suddenly he hears someone laughing, "alien, yet familiar," and sees a man of indeterminate age, "tall, thin, and bearded, with a mocking smile beneath his moustache". He realises that the Rabbi was right when he asked him to come back:

A chance meeting can change the whole world and bring all things into question. Nothing exists purely on its own; past and future can be conceived only as a function of the present, a present which constantly expands and exceeds itself. The simple look of man in a crowd is enough to force a new beginning.

Gregor murmurs the name Gavriel, but the stranger seems neither to see nor hear him, nor does he respond when Gregor reminds him that he saved his life and taught him the value of silence and laughter. Gregor, thinking that Gavriel is mute, asks him only to listen. He begs the man to give back his name so that he can change, "To become again what I was". As the stranger begins asking Gregor questions about his origins, his past and his beliefs, Gregor replies in monosyllables and short sentences, believing that his friend's denial and abandonment means that "you are dead in him as he is dead in you. No more Gavriel. No more Gregor. However, he thinks that perhaps he is mistaken about the identity of the stranger: "This man who resembled Gavriel and now strangely recalled his father was neither". And yet, Gregor feels compelled to tell him stories justifying his own survival, "for being alive instead of buried beneath the ruins". Although the stranger is content to listen, Gregor detects a change in the way he listens:-"You used to live them, by giving them your breath, your solitude, out of which they made love and prayer". Moreover, the stranger does not laugh at his stories.

The story Gregor tells him of his love for Clara is related in the first-person, and appears in italics as chapter 2 in the section "Winter." The narration consists mainly of the dialogues between Gregor and Clara after their chance meeting in Paris after the war. Their incompatible links with the past, held precariously together through the death of Leib, are presented as fragments of conversation, unspoken accusations and unanswered questions around Leib's death and Gregor's betrayal. Neither Gregor, nor Clara are able to come to terms with the past. Gregor's narration of the uneasy relationship between them ends abruptly as the omniscient narrator concludes his story by informing the reader: "Soon after they were married. It was a rainy day, and the Rabbi said, 'That's a good sign '". But their life together is one of anguish. Clara perpetually cries in her sleep for Leib, and Gregor realises that he no longer loves her. He wants to leave her but decides to stay after telling his tale to the stranger. The stranger, whom Gregor calls Gavriel, insists on knowing more than Gregor's list of defeats, but then concedes by saying: "I don't like victories". For the last time in the novel, Gregor implores Gavriel to acknowledge the link between them:

> Speak, Gavriel! Laugh! I want to hear your voice, to have it trace the boundary between you and me, to confirm the fact that I didn't imagine your past or betray my own. (218)

But the stranger remains silent, does not laugh or show any emotion – he merely listens. When he disappears from the tale, Gregor no longer knows to whom he had been talking, whether it was only to a stranger "who had borrowed the features of Gavriel". Only then does Gregor becomes aware that his life in the forest was different, that its simplicity and unity created "no divorce between self and its image, between being and acting". He realises that he can no longer live in a cloistered universe, choosing the path of solitude by shutting the gate leading to humanity. He had been sitting all night on a bench in the Rabbi's house. The stranger was no longer there but in his place Gregor sees a child staring at him who asks him to be the tenth man for the *Minyan*, the morning prayer. The boy asks Gregor his name. At first he gives his name as Gregor, but then corrects himself, saying: "Gavriel. Gavriel's my name. Gregor isn't a Jewish name, you know that". His reply offers a key to the way in which the interchangeable roles and identities of the narrators are finally integrated into one narrative voice. Gregor, by taking back the name of his grandfather, is fulfilling the debt of continuity, a burden the survivor must bear alone.

In his new role as Gavriel, the narrator is able to assume the responsibility of reciting the Kaddish, the prayer for the dead: "the solemn affirmation, filled with grandeur and serenity, by which man returns God his crown and his sceptre". As he concentrates on every word and syllable of the prayer, he suddenly becomes aware of the relationship between death and eternity, between eternity and the word. For the first time, he is able to pray for the soul of his father, God, the soul of his childhood and, "above all, for the soul of his old comrade Leib the Lion, who, during his life, had incarnated what is immortal in man".

There is no conclusion to the novel as the ending is bound to its beginning. Whether the stranger from whom Gregor reclaims his name is Gavriel, or whether the void of Gavriel's disappearance from the forest creates his imaginary presence, is unimportant to the narrative resolution of the novel. The quest, like the unanswered questions and the unopened gates will continue for as long as there is a narrator who can tell the tale with words and silence, and a listener who can hear the silence in the tale. Gavriel's silent presence as both narrator and listener is the predominant narrative strategy Wiesel employs in the narration of *The Gates of the Forest*.

CHAPTER 5
THE SILENCE BETWEEN THE TALES IN
A BEGGAR IN JERUSALEM

Nowhere in Wiesel's fictional universe are his narrators portrayed as more enigmatic, mysterious and shadowy than in a *A Beggar in Jerusalem*. Nor has there been such a gathering of beggars and madmen embodying Jewish history and legend as at the recovered Western Wall in the heart of Jerusalem immediately after the Six-Day War. Wiesel seized upon the events of May-June 1967 and wrote the novel under their immediate impact to capture the unique significance of this war. As André Neher remarks in *The Exile of the Word*, "the granite impressiveness" of these events and those of Auschwitz belong together, not because "one was a compensation for the other, but because time will never be able to erode the significance of either, or the dialectical connection between them, even if they are ultimately both absurd".

A Beggar in Jerusalem is the most demanding of Wiesel's novels because of its narrative structuring, the interweaving of themes, the excursions into the past, the impinging of the past on present events, the deliberate fragmentation, the stories within stories, and the lack of a cohesive and unifying plot. As in most of his fiction, the characters are not defined and cannot be individually identified as they are invariably interchangeable with one another. They are mysterious and mythical night figures who haunt the Wall and exist only in relation to it, to each other and to the stories they tell. But the complexity lies mostly in the multiple narrative voices of the central narrator, David, who not only doubts his own existence as a survivor, but doubts the existence of his friend Katriel for whom he is constantly searching after his mysterious disappearance in the war. David is one of the beggars who "knows how to wait" at the Wall, but whether he is the *Beggar* in the title of the book or whether the title refers to the *mekubal*, the mystical-visionary madman whose presence has haunted Jerusalem for centuries, is a matter of conjecture. In fact, the title may refer to an embodiment of all the beggars in Jerusalem who individually claim they were responsible for winning the war.

The beggars, living in close proximity to the Wailing Wall – those remains of the Second Temple, which Jews pray to be restored – transmit their tales in metaphor and mystery. Each of these timeless and imposing wall-characters refuses to abandon the sacred "city of David," whose holy ground contains the secrets of generations. Jerusalem, "the mysterious city where time no longer counts", is the supreme magical location where messengers, beggars and madmen conjure up the past, speak in prophetic spiritual terms and appear and disappear as matter-of-factly as the movement of the military tanks of the Six-Day War. As David says: "For my part, I gladly acknowledge their place in the haunted history of the city, a thousand times lost and a thousand times recaptured by the madmen, always the same madmen". And, for David, the madmen are always synonymous with the beggars.

The word "beggar" is highly significant for it also means "seeker." As Steinsaltz explains in *Beggars and Prayers*: "By devoting their lives to the quest for sparks of holiness that are immanent in the world yet exiled from it, the beggars are seeking a connection to divinity". Jewish tradition, particularly Hasidic literature, reveals that the beggar may be the prophet Elijah in disguise, a heralder of the Messiah. Like the disguised *Lamed-Vav Tzaddikim*, the thirty-six eternally extant men without whom the world could not be sustained, the Messiah himself is often portrayed in legend as a beggar. It is hardly surprising, given Wiesel's Hasidic background and his immersion in Hasidic legends, that the motif of the beggar is incorporated so prodigiously in his writing. Furthermore, the recurring motif of the beggar is a link in the chain of storytelling that stretches from oral Hasidic tradition to modern fiction.

The difficulty of assessing *A Beggar in Jerusalem* as "a novel of the Six-Day War," as it is described by Wiesel himself, is that the disparate elements in the narration of the story do not fuse together to unify its structure. As Curt Leviant writes:

> The fusion of sub genres and styles (myths, Midrash, folktales, philosophic dialogue, Jewish history, journalism, epigrams) seems artificial. Instead of an organic

> whole we get brilliant fragments. Entire sections are so
> self-contained they could be removed or placed elsewhere
> without doing harm to the narrative. (26)

However, if the novel is assessed as a fictional tale in the Hasidic tradition, this fragmentation and the multiple perspectives intrinsic to its meaning would manifest themselves in a more coherent way. While I will examine the narrative process of this work later in the discussion, taking into account Wiesel's narrative strategies and the way in which his narrators portray silence, I want first to suggest that *A Beggar in Jerusalem* can be read as a continuation of Rabbi Nahman of Bratzlav's unfinished tale of "The Seven Beggars," transcribed a century and a half before the publication of Wiesel's book.[1]

Both stories are complex and ambiguous, containing rich Biblical imagery, Kabbalistic symbols, legendary heroes, parables and folk narrative elements. They have a similar narrative structure in that the stories have both an outer and an inner narrative framework which provides the setting for the beggars to tell their tales. In Nahman's *Tales*, the outer narrative framework consists of the story of the king and his son which is no more than a beginning of a narrative that is never concluded.[2] The inner narrative framework, on the other hand, as in *A Beggar in Jerusalem*, comprises the tales told by the beggars. The combination of these elements and their multiple levels of meaning lend a quality to these tales that can only be described as mythic. By its very nature, myth is a concretisation of abstract truth or notion in narrative form. It has been defined by Arthur Green in *Tormented Master* as "a tale that bespeaks an inner truth portrayed as an ancient truth". As such, it characteristically takes the form of a particularising tale, locating the general notion it wishes to convey in the life of some individual figure who best exemplifies it. In doing so, the myth does not make a claim only about that individual but rather concerning the human situation as reflected in that individual. This theoretical notion can be explained in a simpler way by quoting the beginning of one of Rabbi Nahman's stories, a story Wiesel retells in a different version in *A Beggar in Jerusalem*:

> Once upon a time there was a country that encompassed all the countries of the world. And in the country, there was a town that incorporated all the towns of the country; and in that town there was a street in which were gathered all the streets of the town; and on that street there was a house that sheltered all the houses of the street; and in that house was a room, and in that room there was a man, and that man personified all men of all countries and that man laughed and laughed – no one had ever laughed like that before. (excerpted Edelman, 74)

The telling of tales in itself was of course nothing new in the Hasidic world. From the time of the Ba'al Shem Tov, the Master of the Good Name[3], and down to our own day, Hasidism has been distinguished by its rich traditions of storytelling. Nevertheless, Nahman's tales constituted a major innovation. In the early days of Hasidism, tales were told about the masters rather than by them. Nahman is the author not the subject – at least not ostensibly – of the tales he tells. The vast majority of the Hasidic stories concerned the lives of the tzaddikim, the righteous men; Nahman's tales dealt rather with such figures as bewitched princesses, kings and heroes, wood-spirits and wizards and invariably, mysterious beggars. Nahman's tales partake of the world of fantasy and yet go beyond it, transforming the folk motif and intentional symbolism into myth. However, if there is a single feature of Nahman's tales (indeed of Nahman's life as well), that makes them unique in the history of Judaism it is that their essential motif is the quest. Arthur Green suggests that the tales affirm this endless quest; their central figure searches for the "shekinah," the indwelling presence of God, "wandering through the woods or sailing the seas, stumbling through the kingdom of lies, or flying through the air to reach the tree of life". The sojourns of Nahman's heroes are more than the wandering of the Jew in exile – they become "exhilarating adventures of quest."

Nahman, whose life was that of a seeker, could only define his existence in irreducible sacred symbols or in the ultimate profundities of silence. He said of himself that he was most alone with God when in the midst of people, and that he was capable of crying out in such a way that those around him could hear nothing at all:

> Know that it is possible to let out a very great scream in a still small voice, in such a way that no one will hear. No sound actually comes out – the scream takes place within the silence. Everyone is capable of such a cry. You just imagine the scream in your mind and let its sound penetrate your brain. (excerpted Green, 367)

The cry in Nahman's *Tales* has been redeemed from silence. Nahman the silent screamer also referred to himself as Nahman the dancer, a dancer capable of such delicate movement that no one seeing him would know he had moved at all.

There is a striking similarity between Rabbi Nahman and Elie Wiesel. It is obvious that Wiesel's Hasidic background in Sighet, the town in which he spent his childhood before the deportation of the Jews to Auschwitz, determined his profound love of Jewish mysticism. His vocation as a storyteller, no doubt influenced by the wealth of Hasidic tales he had heard or read, has subsequently led to the retelling of these tales in many of his books. While Rabbi Nahman's tales have not, to my knowledge, been specifically compared to Wiesel's fiction, it seems that much of the mysterious ambiguity, the deliberate paradoxes, the allusive and obscure stories and his choice of enigmatic narrators in Wiesel's fiction are a reflection of the Hasidic master he so admired.

The paradoxical quality of their spiritual temperament led both Nahman and Wiesel to probe the ambiguities of man's inner nature and his warring inclinations toward evil and good. Solitude, silence and laughter are basic narrative themes in their work; but whereas Nahman's "surges of ecstasy" and "paroxysms of anxiety" motivated much of his work, Wiesel's obsession with madness has driven him to make the madman, who may also be the beggar, the hero or narrator of his tales. Nahman, described as the tormented master, believed that liberation through fantasy was possible: the imagination had to be purified so that it could become a vehicle that would lead man back to God. Wiesel, a tormented survivor, believes that liberation through an imaginary past is possible, if the imagination can become a vehicle to bear witness to the unburied dead, lest they be forgotten by God and man. Both authors are seekers and their tales are a series of quests. But while Nahman's tales sought to restore his listeners to the life of dream and take them on a journey through the world of fantasy, Wiesel's tales seek to restore his readers to the world of the dead and take them on a journey into the past.

In Wiesel's *A Beggar in Jerusalem*, the gathering of the beggars at the Wall of the Old City is reminiscent of Nahman's assembly of beggars at the wedding feast in the tale of "The Seven Beggars." In Wiesel's narrative the celebration marks the victory of the Six-Day War and the rejoining of the Western Wall to the heart of Israel. In Nahman's tale the celebration represents the restoration of harmony after a catastrophe in which only two children survived. Their marriage would provide a new generation and a fresh start for humanity. In each of the narratives the beggars tell fantastic tales of their exploits and prowess in a particular sphere. All Nahman's beggars have individual deformities that characterise them, but they are only apparent defects. Whereas they are perceived externally as faults they are really qualities that are intrinsically perfect. The blind beggar has an acuity of vision so great that he does not perceive the details of mundane existence; the deaf beggar is unable to hear the vanities and troubles of the world; the speech of the beggar who stutters is so lofty that other men could only hear fragments of it; the hunchback beggar who apparently can bear nothing on his back holds quality rather than quantity; and the sixth beggar who has no hands can retrieve an arrow after it has struck its prey. The seventh beggar, who has no feet, does not arrive at the wedding feast. He is thought to represent the Biblical King David whose dancing is described in the second book of Samuel. Dancing is of great significance in Hasidic celebrations, as dance, in bringing together all the powers of the feet, represents the basis of simple and perfect faith. I would suggest that the seventh beggar in Nahman's tale, the legless dancer, who does not tell his tale, is brought back into Wiesel's story as its central narrator. It is possible that Wiesel may have considered the triumph of the Six-Day War an ideal setting to continue Nahman's unfinished tale.

In *A Beggar in Jerusalem*, at nightfall, in the shadow of the Wall, Wiesel's beggars tell their tales, recounting their exploits during the War, and "If they are to be believed, the entire victory was their doing". Ezra ben Abraham, an old man from Morocco, claims that it was his tears that made victory possible: "From the first day to the last I did nothing but weep. And it worked". Velvel, the one eyed beggar with a glib tongue disagrees vehemently saying that it was his rejoicing that turned the enemy back: "I never stopped dancing, even while eating, even while sleeping". Zadok, an emaciated Yemenite, pronounces that victory was achieved through his continuous praying, night and day; while Moshe the madman, proclaims that it was his singing and laughter that drowned out the sound of the cannons and "all the noises of the earth, all the regrets of mankind". Yakov the Timid ventures his part in the victory which he believes was brought about by the war games he played with the children to alleviate their fear. And the blind beggar, Shlomo the Seer, whose blindness does not prevent him from seeing himself, safeguards his secret and continues to wait for an unknown figure that has not yet appeared in Jerusalem. He says that here, "more than anywhere else, waiting cries out for meaning, even if at first there was none". These pursuits of the beggars, whether they are through prayer, song, dance, laughter or in the act of waiting for the Messiah, are highly significant in Hasidic life as they contribute to the ethical values of individual existence as well as to the religious fervour of the community.

But it is in the telling of tales that Hasidism finds its true expression. In the novel, Dan the Prince, "a vagabond and liar of considerable talent" weaves a fantastic story of his journey to an enchanted kingdom, beyond the mythical river Sambatyon, which separates the Ten Lost Tribes of Israel from the world. His heroic deeds in that magical domain elevated him to the rank of a prince. His return to

Jerusalem, as an emissary for the king "on a mission of unprecedented importance" contributes to the favourable outcome of the war. Before the outbreak of hostilities, he bombarded cabinet ministers, politicians, generals and columnists with offers of financial and military aid, which, although he admits they went unanswered, led to the optimism that accompanied victory. While his legendary exploits ignite the imagination of his rapt audience; it is his role as messenger that is most significant for David: "All of us are messengers. If man is the messenger of man, why should a madman not be the messenger of God".

While David is the protagonist of the novel and the first-person narrator, the tales of the beggars which fragment his narration are crucial to the way in which silence is created and sustained throughout the work. In "the city of unshakeable memory" the beggars' tales are the link between the legendary past, Hasidic tradition, and the immediacy of the Six-Day War. As Yakov the Timid says: "This is where words and silence come to terms". The beggars, both narrators and listeners, appear and disappear, giving them a dimension of timelessness and invincibility. David's own involvement with his search for Katriel is given the same credibility as Dan's journey to his legendary kingdom, Itzhik's war adventures and ben Abraham's encounter with "a terrible and powerful sultan." The beggars are tellers of tales: "What they have to transmit they do with silence as much as with words". Their lives, their stories and silences are interwoven and interchangeable and moreover can never be resolved, having like the novel itself no beginning and no ending.

The opening paragraph of *A Beggar in Jerusalem* epitomises the mysticism and allusive ambiguity of the narrator's role in the telling of his tale:

> The tale the beggar tells must be told from the beginning.

> But the beginning has its own tale, its own secret. That's
> how it is, and that's how it has always been. There is
> nothing man can do about it. Death itself has no power
> over the beginning. The beggar who tells you this knows
> what he is talking about. (3)

The identity of that beggar is never disclosed but the reader is asked to participate in finding out who he is: "Do you see him? There. Sitting on a tree stump ... Don't ask him, he won't answer: he hates answers". From the outset, the narrator sets up a paradoxical situation in which he establishes an intimacy between himself and the reader, who takes on the role of the listener in the tale, thus creating the illusion of shared experience. At the same time his intangible presence makes it difficult for the listener to expect any consistency in his narration. He poses rhetorical and unanswerable questions to which silence will be the only appropriate response. The narrator, who is like a storyteller in Hasidic oral tradition, coaxes his audience to be patient and to come closer to the beggar who will not cast a spell over them: "He is beckoning. Do you see him now? It is he. It is I". The narrator may be talking of himself, or Katriel, who "dead or alive" will claim his place in the tale; or he may be referring to any one of the beggars who wait at the Wall. The narrative strategy of introducing David as the first-person narrator and then continually questioning his existence adds to the mysterious aura surrounding the teller and his tale. It also increases the tenuous relationship he has with his listener to whom he confides that "he is sure of nothing. Not even the moment which unites us, you and me" Furthermore, his role as a beggar is not what it seems: "He neither begs nor asks for anything, either from man or from God".

Just as the narrator is expelled from time and prefers to

avoid the present, the listener is urged to follow his imaginary journeys into the past even while being constantly reminded that the tale is being unfolded in the real world of Jerusalem immediately after the events of the Six-Day War. David's memory, however, takes him back to the other post-war period in Europe after the Holocaust where he was one of the survivors who were not allowed victory: "We were beggars, unwanted everywhere, condemned to exile and reminding strangers everywhere of what they had done to us and to themselves". Feeling rejected by both the living and the dead, David decides to return to his native town without knowing what he hopes to find there. He learns that only three survivors of the Jewish community escaped deportation and that they were committed to the insane asylum. He is only able to communicate with the youngest patient who tells David his story of his madness:

> Imagine the unimaginable. Imagine my seeing this town without its Jews. It sounds inconceivable, I know. And yet that is how I see it, as distinctly as you see me now.... Where are the talkative tailors, the haughty doctors, the rich merchants and their customers, the wedding minstrels and the brides-to-be, the frenzied beggars and the secret "tzaddikim" disguised as beggars? Where are the Masters of silences pregnant with meaning, and their disciples, where are they? ... They are here, I know, though invisible and strangely wrapped in absence.(24-25)

The young madman, convinced that the hallucinations of his tormented mind are self-imposed, pleas with David to pronounce the words that will extricate him from his madness. But David does not answer. The silence then, broken by the old men's insane laughter, remains with the narrator and his listeners long after the tale is told.

Thereafter, the narrator shifts the focus and returns to the immediate present by describing the sunset in Jerusalem. Again he establishes an almost teasing intimacy with his listener by evoking the name of Katriel and then withdrawing it by saying, "Do not ask me who he is, I will not tell you, not yet". The scene returns to the Wall and the fragmented tales the beggars tell. Moshe, the madman, is drunk and tells of the girl he once loved, as well as his encounter with the Prophet Elijah who was said to have told him that laughter "in itself is a miracle, the most astonishing miracle of all". Itzhik, a truck driver, tells a story out of the immediate present, while Zalmen expounds on his part in the Bar Kochba revolt against Rome. The narrator explains, almost apologetically, that his companions are not speechmakers: "They are tellers of tales. What they have to transmit they do with silence as much as with words".

In spite of the multiple narrative voices in the novel, and the seeming hesitancy of the central narrator to tell his own story, there is a pattern that emerges in the narrative process. While time is fluid and the boundaries between imagination and reality dissolve, and the beggars in Hasidic legend merge with the beggars in Jerusalem, the silence between the tales becomes the unifying strategy in the structure of the work. The constant shifts in time and place, the unresolved questions, the intangible presence of Katriel, the unfinished tales and the testimony of the messengers and madmen, create the space for silence as a narrative device, as well as permitting the narrator to be silent when words are no longer needed to fill in the gaps and the pauses. Silence also serves to build up the narrative suspense of the central plot revolving around the narrator's meeting with Katriel and his passive participation in the Six-Day War.

His visit to Lieutenant Colonel Gad's headquarters is narrated in a matter-of-fact reportorial style. Gad, overworked, on edge, "harried by his superiors, harassed by his subordinates," hardly has the time or patience for his friend's strange request to join the army and go to the war front. The opportunity arises when one of the men in a combat unit is hospitalised and David seizing on this coincidence manages to persuade Gad to allow him to replace the missing man. He does not continue with the story until Chapter 8, half way through the book, and resumes it only after the reader has become acquainted (through the omniscient narrator) with Katriel, his wife Malka and their dead son, Sasha. The third person narration of the night before Katriel goes to war and takes leave of his wife is inserted prior to David's meeting with him, as though to ensure the veracity of Katriel's existence, which the narrator himself continually doubts.

The first-person narrator, David, who is now in army uniform, continues the narrative in the same journalistic style that characterised his interlude with Gad. He has to explain to the members of his unit that although he is standing in for a gunner, he has never touched a gun in his life. He is neither serving in Intelligence nor is he engaged on active duty. He is not a member of the Reserves, and has not been mobilised in any other capacity. He can only tell them that he is a Jew, and he will be "looking around." As the soldiers roar with laughter at his outrageous reasons for being involved in the war, Katriel comes forward and introduces himself to David. He tells the soldiers that they must not laugh: "Looking and telling are neither easier nor less important than the rest". While the soldiers accept Katriel's explanation, they voice their disapproval of his silence in their camp. And Katriel is forced to speak up and defend his silence although his speech is like that "of a sick man struggling to live and to speak." He admits that, "I am as responsible for my silence as you are for your words". The men, thunderstruck at the miracle of Katriel' ability to speak, become, with David, the rapt audience for Katriel's story, which contains the crucial message of the narrative process in the novel:

> I love stories, and it is thanks to my father that I love them. Everything I know I learned from him. He taught me to measure myself against my words and to attune myself to their silence if not always to the truth they conceal; he taught me how to listen. Do you know that it is given to us to enrich a legend simply by listening to it? It belongs as much to the listener as to the teller. You listen to a tale, and all of a sudden it is no longer the same tale . . . . Do you realise that it is in our power to deepen the source by simply moving toward it? That too I learned from my father. I am just repeating his words. But the silence within my words is my own. (107)

That silence is communicated by the narrator's following comments: "He stopped. Entranced, the men did nothing, said nothing which might break the spell". Until that day Katriel had not spoken.

A few days later David makes a pact with Katriel that whichever one of them survives will bear witness for the other. Katriel tries to dissuade David by saying that he does not know anything about him, that words destroy what they aim to describe and alter what they try to emphasise. But David, convinced that it will be Katriel who will testify for him, and that their roles are interchangeable, assures him that he does know him: he knows his questions, his tales, the way he talks, listens and watches, as well as his passion for mystery and silence. Although he concedes that these are only elements in his personality, "Together they make up what you are, each expressing a particular aspect". When Katriel disappears, almost at the same time as Gad is killed, and shortly after they have had their first glimpse at the Wall when Jerusalem is liberated, it is Katriel's silence in the mad, joyous shouting that continues to haunt David's life and memory.

Like the young madman in the insane asylum, David feels that Katriel's presence "though invisible and wrapped in absence", reflects a vision of reality that is hallucinatory. Even his meeting with Katriel's wife seems to him to have been an hallucination. Sitting at the Wall, as midnight approaches, exchanging stories with the other beggars, Katriel sees a female silhouette moving with "dreamlike grace" toward him. She mysteriously knows David's name, although it could not have been Katriel who told her. When the beggars ask her why Katriel is not with them, she answers, "Who is Katriel?". In spite of the beggars being witnesses, Katriel's very existence is questioned once more. Malka, whom the beggars call their "queen," then disappears from the story and reappears, perhaps at another meeting with David. For the narrator, as with the beggars, chronological time has no meaning, and the listener has to adjust to the timelessness of the tale by disregarding the sequence of the story. When Malka offers her love to David, he asks her to dance with him "to change the order of the night and its disorder as well". But suddenly, Malka's eyes became the eyes of Ileana who sacrificed her life to save David. Malka now becomes associated with his forbidden memories. At this point, the narrator again inserts a story-within-a story that has little to do with Katriel, the war, or even the beggars, and serves only to fragment his narrative by bringing back memories of his own survival. The present and the past merge as

Katriel's wife becomes interchangeable with Ileana, a woman he once loved and watched die.

Towards the end of the novel, Malka becomes the narrator's listener and it is she who asks David to give up the past, telling him that "The dead have no right in Jerusalem". But David is neither convinced that Katriel will not reappear one day under another identity, "more mysterious and more invincible" than before, nor is he able to distinguish between Katriel's memories and stories and those of his own. They are inextricably intertwined, and whether Katriel is alive or not is unimportant to David because his disappearance would prove nothing except that "certain stories don't have an ending. Or a beginning". And "the beggar knows how to wait". He tells Malka, or perhaps he is addressing his remarks to his unknown listeners, that it is his memory and the unanswered questions that keep him in the haunted square beside the Wall, "in this city where nothing is lost and nothing dispersed":

> While accepting ambiguity and the quest arising from it, the beggar at times would like to lose his memory; he can not. On the contrary: it keeps growing and swelling, storing away events and faces until the past of others becomes one with his own. By continued survival, he no longer differentiates between his allies, his ghosts and his guides, and whether he owes them allegiance. For him everything is question, including the miracle that keeps him on the surface. (210)

The beggar is always the link between Katriel and David, the past and the present, imagination arid reality. David remembers Katriel's reminiscences of his part in the siege of the Old City twenty years previously, when he encountered a beggar, who may have been a "mekubal," a mystical madman or a visionary who haunted the Old City for centuries. Katriel believed that he remained behind, "hiding in the confines of his invisible kingdom". When David sees the army chaplain approaching the Wall carrying the Torah, like "a bridegroom on his wedding day," he wonders where he had seen him before; whether he was the beggar, the preacher of his childhood, King David, Abraham, Katriel or the Messiah. Like Nahman's *Tales*, *A Beggar in Jerusalem* expresses in narrative form the life of a world beyond any ordinary sequence of time and space. When the stories lose that certain mysterious ambiguity they cease to be myth. Just as Nahman's seven beggars may be thought to represent Biblical figures, Talmudic sages or even different aspects of Nahman himself, so Wiesel's beggars can be interpreted as legendary heroes in Hasidic lore, real or imaginary madmen of his childhood, messengers of the unburied dead or witnesses to the redemption of Israel. Any univalent interpretation of the stories limiting their multiple levels of meaning would rob them of their richness of ambiguity. It is for this reason that the most satisfying reading of *A Beggar in Jerusalem*, whether it is seen in the context of the Hasidic tradition or is assessed as a modern novel of the Six-Day War, is that the narrative process of the tale should be considered as essential to its meaning as the themes that are explored in the text. In this novel Wiesel offers to his reader as many interpretations as the multiple narrative voices of his central narrator allow. It is only in the telling of the tale that the silence can be heard, and it is the beggar who ultimately is able to convey the timelessness of that silence.

There is no ending to the tale of *A Beggar in Jerusalem*. The last sentence of the novel brings its circular narrative process back to the beginning: "For tales, like people, all have the same beginning". As André Neher remarks: "The last word of the book is an orphaned word: it is the word 'beginning.' It has been wrenched away from its companion, the end". But in the telling of their tales and between their tales, the beggars of Jerusalem bring silence "where it is needed, when it is needed".

CHAPTER 6
THE SILENCE OF THE NARRATORS IN
THE OATH

In his book *Against the Apocalypse*, David Roskies convincingly argues that there is a collective memory of Jewish historical tragedy which forms a traditional response to catastrophe. He shows that the force of recurrent catastrophe acts as a crucible in which all prior responses are refined and recombined. He states: "The Jewish dialectic response is at the core a profoundly neo-classical impulse: the greater the catastrophe, the more its victims reshape the ancient archetypes.(11)" By examining the liturgy of destruction of the First and Second Temples, the lamentation literature of the Bible, the poetry during and after the Eastern European pogroms, the literary output in response to "the rape of the *shtetl,*" and the writings of the ghetto, Roskies discovers that there is an historical continuity in the Jewish literature of destruction. He maintains that even when examining the qualitative difference of the Holocaust catastrophe claims can be made to continuity in the literary themes and archetypes of destruction. His assumption is that: "If the Holocaust is a break, then the subsequent work about it should either attempt to capture it by entirely new modes, or face the break in great confusion". In the examples he cites of the Jewish writers of Eastern Europe, he finds that while their styles may be new, the process is the same. He suggests therefore, that the historical break was anticipated by the artistic process, especially after World War 1, so that despite the disappearance of a culture, its means of handling catastrophe lingers on.

One can neither deny the validity of Roskies' proposition, based on brilliant insight and careful scrutiny, particularly of the Yiddish and Hebrew writers of the twentieth century, nor can one fail to recognise the merit of Sidra DeKoven Ezrahi's comprehensive and invaluable study *By Words Alone*, in which she takes a stance in opposition to Roskies' conclusions. She finds that although Holocaust literature is a reflection of recent history, it cannot draw upon timeless archetypes of human experience and behaviour. Her evaluation of post-Holocaust writers shows that the development of the creative literature is the least consistent with traditional moral and artistic conventions precisely where it is most confined to the unimaginable facts of violence and horror. It is Ezrahi's contention that: "Even the most vivid presentation of concrete detail and specificity, the most palpable reconstruction of Holocaust reality, is blinded by the fact that there is no analogue in human experience". In drawing a distinction between a collective literature and a "displaced" literature, she holds the view that for a writer set adrift by the Nazis from the source of life's continuity, the reference is usually private experience rather than the more generalised historical question of collective identity and destiny. Her conclusions lead to the underlying assumptions of Holocaust literature, namely that the pre-eminent role of Holocaust art is testimony. As an act of commemoration the survivor needs to bear witness and does this from personal experience.

While in many respects Roskies' and Ezrahi's proposals may appear to be contradictory for the critical evaluation of post Holocaust writers, both views can be accommodated in testimonial literature, and particularly in Wiesel's fictional universe. *The Oath*, Wiesel's seventh novel, is one of the best examples in his fiction of a work that provokes ambiguities, sets up antimonies, suggests alternatives and finally leaves the questions open-ended. Wiesel's ability to note dualities, to embrace none or both, allows the reader to become aware of continuities, parallels, separations, disjunctions, perpetual beginnings and inconclusions. Wiesel achieves these various levels of paradox not only through the contentious themes in the novel but through the narrative strategies he employs. It is his choice of narrators that finally provide the key to the multilevel meanings of the book. By allowing one of his narrators in a specific context to recall traditional archetypal modes, he is able to defend a response to catastrophe on a continuum. At the same time, another narrator in a similar context, can advocate discontinuity by denying the efficacy of a neoclassical response to catastrophe. Moreover, Wiesel sets up a situation where there is only one survivor left to bear witness, yet imposes on him the oath of silence, considering this to be the only kind of testimony that is appropriate for the massacre of Kolvillág.

For the first time in his fiction, Wiesel is confronting a problem not only of the inadequacy of language to express the inexpressible, but is questioning whether language as testimony should be used at all. He is attempting to resolve an extreme paradox of expressing silence through language in order to show the possibility of communicating in silence without language. From this vantage point, it is no longer a question of how to tell the story but how not to tell it. By making the central issue of the novel the abdication of the word, Wiesel is embarking on a project that challenges the written and spoken word, the only tool of literary communication. The subsequent narration of the story would therefore, be a contradiction in terms. It will be my suggestion that while the overall impression of the story is one that is forbidden to be told, and *The Oath* of silence is the prevailing theme of the novel, Wiesel is able to sustain the paradox by imposing varying degrees of silence on his narrators through the narrative process.

The opening paragraph of *The Oath*, is a refusal by the storyteller to tell the tale:

> No, said the old man. I will not speak. What I have to say,
> I don't care to say. Not to you, not to anybody. Not now,
> not tomorrow. There is no tomorrow. (3)

Yet, the novel is a denial of those statements. The old man does speak, he does tell the story to his listener, he does care what he has to say, and there is a promise of tomorrow. But in the narration of the tale, the old man does not lose his credibility. In the way in which he unfolds his story to the reader, he is able to transmit the overwhelming silence within the story through alternating narrative voices, shifts in points of view, excursions into the past and returns to the present. Furthermore, it is in the interrelationship of the narrators that the cessation of speech is most fully realised.

The novel begins as a third person narrative, with the authorial narrator creating a distance between himself and the old man. The words of the old man have the effect of arousing the interest and curiosity of the reader as to why he refuses to speak. At the beginning of an italicised section, immediately following the words of the old man, the listener, the young man, assumes the role of the first person narrator, thus establishing an *in persona* identification with the reader. It is the new narrator who fulfils the reader's expectation by providing some information in the more conventional format of storytelling, particularly that of myth or legend. He begins: "Once upon a time, long, long ago, there was a small town with a mysterious past, a black stain under a purple sky. It's name in Hungarian is Kolvillág . . . .". He proceeds to authenticate the existence of Kolvillág by offering scanty pieces of information discovered in his research: a letter dated in 1822, the correspondence of an obscure Romanian monk, a diary of a sage who held court there in the sixteenth century and the liturgical writings of a poet in the year 5206. The effect of these vague hints of unimportant detail firmly establishes the old man's crucial role as a storyteller, and as the only link with the history of a town that no longer appears on the map. The young listener is aware that he will only be able to learn the secret of Kolvillág through the voice of the last survivor, whose name is Azriel, "and he is mad".

The authorial narration, interrupted by the musings of the young man, and the introduction of the first person narration of the old man, has the effect of an unconsummated dialogue. The reader is often left confused as to who is speaking and from which point of view the story is hesitantly and reluctantly being unfolded. In addition, the frequent changes in tense add to the confusion of the reader: the old man speaks of the past as though it is present, and the young man speaks of the present as though it is in the past. While the first section of the book "The Old Man and the Child" has three narrators, it would seem feasible to assume that the function of the authorial narrator would be to link the first person narrations of Azriel and the young man. However, it rarely achieves this because the authorial intervention is never sufficiently sustained to add a further dimension to the disparate stories.

The name of the young man remains undisclosed throughout the book. Through his haunting and recurring recollections of his mother's perpetual suffering with the loss of her first child in the concentration camps, the reader is able to infer that the young narrator is the child of survivors. His anonymity is not only a reflection of the survivors who lost their names in "the Kingdom of Night," but of the generation after, who began life without a past. Because of the burden of his mother's past and his exclusion from the Holocaust experience, his existence as an usurper, an unwanted replacement for his dead brother, becomes untenable and leads to his decision to end his own life. His only memory is that of his dying mother whom he could not help. The young man does not speak of his predicament nor of his life which remains, with his name shrouded in silence. His encounter with Azriel, gives him a reason to live as he becomes obsessed with the need to discover Azriel's past, a past with which he can identify and adopt as his own. He says: "By allowing me to enter his life, he gave meaning to mine," making it possible for him "to dwell in two places" and claim "more than one role" as his own. Although the young man's presence is important in the first part of the book because it establishes him as the recipient of the story, infrequent reference is made of him subsequently. The old man occasionally refers to him as "my boy" as a reminder to the reader that he is still part of the story. It is only in the concluding page of the novel that the young man's voice is heard again, reinforcing the idea that his absence from the narrative is more like a silent presence. Thus, the reader feels obliged to take over or at least share his role as listener.

In the same way as the reader is able to piece together a vague sketch of the young man through Azriel's vacillating interior monologues, so a blurred impressionistic portrait of the old man emerges from the musing of the young man, who has gathered odd accounts of him through people to whom he has spoken. The old man's life as a wanderer for fifty years after leaving Kolvillág is steeped in mystery, and adds to the enigmatic quality of the storyteller who may be a saint, a madman or "a Just man disguised as a vagabond". The young man discovers that nobody has succeeded in knowing him nor could they recall his physical features. Each person describes him in a different and contradictory way. It appears that Azriel is "equally at ease quoting from the Talmud or Mao Tse Tung; he mastered seven ancient languages and a dozen living ones". He had taught philosophy to professional philosophers and had lectured to tycoons on the stock market. The descriptions of Azriel seem to embrace all facets of life and encompass his ability to commune with all people.

Through his stories, the young man is able to glimpse at some areas in Azriel's life which are like "a hyphen between countless communities". The youth is told about Rachel whom the old man loved because she was able to make him laugh, and about his friendship with a revolutionary activist, Abrasha, whose dream was communism, which he believed would abolish "evil and suffering, hunger and poverty, social injustice and war". Azriel recounts an incident where he is taken for a miracle maker, "a Just Man," to help the poor, heal the sick, and restore health to the afflicted. As the crowd gathers around him, pleading with him to use his powers to alleviate their suffering, he chooses "escape into laughter" which convinces them that he is indeed "a divine messenger". During many visits to synagogues in various communities he is always asked to deliver a sermon. On each occasion he can only say: "I am here not to speak but to hold my tongue". Wherever he goes the speaker became speechless.

The only irrefutable fact the reader is able to ascertain about Azriel is his obsession to save the life of the young man, "not to offer death one more victim". He tells him stories, preaches to him, makes him eat, drink, walk and speak because, as he ironically notes, "one does not commit suicide in the middle of a sentence". He attempts to make the young man dream, to invite a future and deny death because again, "One doesn't kill oneself while dreaming". But Azriel knows that the only sure way to save the young man's life is to tell him the story of Kolvillág, to break the oath of silence "not only to save you but also to save myself". He says the following words silently to himself:

> I'll transmit my experience to him and he, in turn will be compelled to do the same. He in turn will become a messenger. And once a messenger, he has no alternative. He must stay alive until he has transmitted his message.
> (33)

Before allowing the narrators to tell the tale of Kolvillág, Wiesel inserts a story-within-a-story that is crucial for an understanding of the way in which the story is transmitted without speech. It is not clear whether Azriel narrates the story to the young man or whether it is contained in his silent imaginary journeys into the past. He recalls his visit to Rabbi Zusia of Kolomey, an extraordinary Hasidic rabbi, to whom his disciples could entrust their souls, and to whom "you could reveal what you tried to conceal from yourself". After spending Shabbat in his court and antagonising the Hasidim because of his sadness and his refusal to rejoice, the rabbi severely reprimands him: "There is no room under this roof for anyone who cannot control his sorrow and prevent it from affecting his fellowman". Azriel implores the rabbi to advise him whether he should speak or remain silent "without turning my silence into a lie or betrayal". The rabbi angrily forbids him to violate his oath, but then concedes, and says:

> I shall listen to you. In my own way, not yours. Without words. I shall listen to what they conceal. You will look straight into my eyes and you will tell me everything. Without moving your lips, without thinking about the words you will use. You will relive everything before me, and the old man and you will become one. Go on, begin. (42)

And so, Azriel opens his mouth without speaking and begins to relive and rethink the events of Kolvillág. The rabbi listens in silence to the tale.

The mute testimony of Azriel is one of Wiesel's most powerful evocations of silence in his fiction. The brevity of a few succinct phrases conjures up a multitude of visual images. The story which is not verbalised at this point, has a far greater impact on the reader than the story which is finally told at length. The fire is more luminous without words, and the end of Kolvillág is more final without language. The story is a dramatic enactment of an abstract notion of a voiceless narrative, a speechless tale. Added to this, is the presence of the mystical rabbi as well as the eloquent silence of Hasidic teaching. After listening to the story, Rebbe Zusia remains silent in deep thought before finally committing Azriel to become a *Na-Venadnik*, a wanderer in perpetual exile, "a stranger among strangers," and "the silence between words".

As in most of Wiesel's novels the central action of the plot serves as a framework or a backdrop to the various levels of meaning in the text. It is never an end in itself, and in *The Oath*, the longest and most fully developed work of fiction he has written thus far, the story is a means of exploring the dialectic between language and silence through various narrative strategies.

The story of *The Oath* is neither original nor extraordinary, and is not unlike any other story of a pogrom in Eastern Europe. It concerns a familiar world of anti-Semitism involving medieval accusations of Jewish ritual murder of a Christian child. The ancient superstition sets in motion a chain reaction of hatred and revenge which culminates in the destruction of the Jewish community. The pogrom takes place in Kolvillág, a town in the Carpathian mountains, shortly before Easter, in the 1920's. It follows an archetypal pattern: a gentile youth, in this case a hoodlum called Yancsi, feared and disliked by the townspeople disappears "mysteriously." The Christian community turn to the "simple" explanation that the Jews of the town have killed him. Thereafter, the events leading to the apocalypse are played out according to the rules set down centuries before. Not even the futile gesture of Moshe, the madman who confesses to the murder, can avert the inevitability of the pogrom. The story is almost a cliché and the stock characters in the action are interchangeable with all victims and oppressors in all pogroms, the time and place being incidental on the continuum of Jewish historical tragedy. As the narrator notes, nothing has changed since the first "ritual murder."

There is no pretence in the narration of the story to introduce exceptional circumstances, provide different motivations for revenge, offer other versions of the massacre, or establish a new archetype or paradigm of destruction. The images of ancient pogroms reappear: smashed doors, shattered windows, broken dishes, "a crushed cat, a trampled rooster," "the sobs and death rattles of the tortured," and "the howling and laughing invaders . . . sowing terror". The events of this pogrom are hardly distinguishable from the accounts of pogroms in the Middle Ages. As Roskies states: "Violence was a built-in feature of Jewish life, a permanent albeit unpredictable part of cyclical time". Why then is this story forbidden to be told? It is my contention that it is precisely because of its familiarity, because of the violent deeds of death and horror which inexorably unfold in a traditional archetypal mode, that Wiesel is able to use the story as a device to explore new and innovative versions of response to catastrophe.

The narration of the pogrom of Kolvillág begins in the second part of the novel, "The Child and the Madman," and continues through Part 3, "The Madman and the Book." It appears to be a predominantly first-person narrative, Azriel being the central narrator who experiences the fictional events. However, it is not only his narrative voice or point of view that is presented to the reader. In the narrative process Wiesel creates the tension by evoking opposing narrative voices that take on the roles of narrator. The titles of the three parts of the book are a key to their identity. In the first section, "The Old Man and the Child," the co-narrators are Azriel and the young man, whereas in the second part, the child is Azriel himself, at about the same age as the listener in Part 1, and the madman is Moshe, who is ultimately responsible for the story of *The Oath*. In the last section, "The Madman and the Book," the Madman is again Moshe who is now the silent narrator, while the Book represents the written testimony of the scribe, Shmuel, the father of Azriel.

The pivotal character in *The Oath*, upon whom the dramatic action revolves, is Moshe the Madman, a figure who appears in different guises and roles throughout Wiesel's fiction. In this novel, he is the composite of all mad Moshes, appearing first in *Night* as the original witness and yet again in *The Oath*, where he reverses his standpoint by denouncing the right of the survivor to bear witness. All the descriptions of him are purposefully vague and mysterious which give an added impetus to his climactic role as the protagonist in *The Oath*. It is Moshe, "a madman unlike any other", to whom Wiesel entrusts his most cogent rationale for using silence as a means to avert further Jewish catastrophe.

The impact of Moshe's sermon is achieved through the narrative strategies Wiesel employs in building up the image of the extraordinary and mystical seer. In Part 1 of the novel, Azriel frequently evokes his name, begging the madman to release him from his oath of silence. Moshe's name, his story and his madness become synonymous with the hidden meaning of Kolvillág. Moreover, as the story progresses, the identity of Moshe the Madman, and Azriel the storyteller, become so intertwined that their narrative voices are invariably interchangeable. However, it is Azriel who furnishes the reader with the only physical description of Moshe. This is delivered in unfinished sentences and staccato phrases: "Moshe, forty or so. Haggard. Unkempt, bushy beard. Sombre, haunted eyes. Intimidating and intimidated, harmless. Subject to depressions, alternate fits of rage and enthusiasm". Azriel gives more attention to Moshe's eyes, remembering how he fell under the spell of the inaccessible when, as a young man of sixteen, he was Moshe's only pupil, elevated to the rank of disciple: "Strange eyes, dark and red – oddly staring, unfathomable. Eyes that went straight to the core of things, seeing nothing but their essence . . . .". These descriptions are hardly sufficient for reinforcing the reader's expectation of the characteristics usually attributable to a protagonist in a novel. The narrative device of withholding detail through the reduction of language allows only the essentials to be presented for interpretation. However, by endowing Moshe with magical powers of being able to see through masks, discover hidden truths and uncover the inner secrets of members of the community, Wiesel gives him the status of a legendary hero, whom people from surrounding villages came to admire and stare at "as though he had three eyes and two mouths". But when Moshe delivers his first sermon at the synagogue, he begs the congregants to allow him to attain his goal through solitude and silence without encumbering him with their worship and curiosity. He shuns all recognition and affection bestowed on him as a saint and true *tzaddik*.

The dramatisation of events leading up to his second sermon are centred around Moshe's martyrdom and torture in prison after he has offered himself as Yancsi's murderer. He realises then that words, as contained in his three word confession "I did it," are futile; that words will not defuse the onslaught of the pogrom, nor, as he thought, change the destiny of Kolvillág. Moshe insists on addressing the community from the pulpit of the ancient synagogue. The tension mounts as the community gathers to listen to "the madman turned saint, or the saint gone mad" because "none other than Moshe, at no other moment in his life" could draw the crowds and create the kind of awesome silence he commands: "He communicated his silence, drawn from the source of his being, even before he translated it into language". When he begins to speak from the depth of silence, his listeners are hardly aware he is speaking, as the sound of his voice is almost like a sigh, a wordless prayer. His rationale begins with the idea that in Jewish history there has always been one storyteller, one survivor, one witness to revive the past and to tell the tale of catastrophe. He explains that words have been the only weapon against death, but because they have been intrinsically linked with hate and destruction, they must be abolished to forestall future ordeals:

> We shall innovate, do what our ancestors and forbears could not or dared not do. We are going to impose the ultimate challenge, not by language but by the absence of language, not by the word but by the abdication of the word . . . . Let us take the only possible decision: we shall testify no more. (239)

Moshe does not ask but orders the community to take the oath of silence under the sign of *Herem*, a word charged with occult powers and evoking eternal damnation. Each member of the community swears the oath accompanied by ancient ritual formulas of anathema, that if the oath is broken, the excommunicated renegade will forfeit his right to belong to any human family, living or dead. The ritual associated with the swearing of the oath is the climax to the central part of the novel. It is also one of Wiesel's most dramatic scenes in his fiction where silence, and not the words about silence, is communicated to the reader. Thereafter, in Part 3, the inevitable massacre of the community of Kolvillág follows, leaving Azriel as the only survivor and witness to carry not only the burden of memory but the severity of the ritual oath never to reveal what he has seen or heard.

Although Moshe is the pivotal character and one of the central narrators in *The Oath*, the role of Shmuel, the chronicler of Kolvillág, is crucial; not only as an opposing narrative voice in the conflict between silence and language, but in the resolution of the story. Whereas Moshe advocates discontinuity through the abdication of the word, thus refuting a response to catastrophe on a continuum, Shmuel insists on the traditional neo-classical response of drawing on ancient archetypes to assure continuity for future generations. Both are witnesses to catastrophe, but Moshe is committed to silencing testimony, while Shmuel is determined to preserve and transmit testimony through the written word. On a broader level, Roskies notes that the Jewish poets responding to the pogroms of Eastern Europe were "caught between acquiescence to an inherited tradition of response, which seemed only too viable – and rebellion against it, if only to break out of the vicious cycle".

Shmuel is the traditional scribe and guardian of the Book, the "Pinkas," the communal archive of Kolvillág. His complete identification with the town and his passionate need to testify in order to protect the sacredness of the Book is described by Azriel in Part 1, and in fact is the only description of him provided to the listener:

> My father loved to write, erase, erase some more, condense twenty words into a single word or preferably into a comma. Did he suffer? Surely. But he was too proud to show it. His life? Total identification with the heroes and characters of the "pinkas," his only reading matter. Look at his legible, precise handwriting. Every sentence is definitive. He chiselled his words and fitted them like stones into a gigantic tower, until they burst apart, like so many dismembered bodies tumbling into the precipice.(79)

When Yancsi disappears, it is Shmuel who tells Azriel that a Christian child who runs away is of more concern to the Jewish community than to his parents: "We have the history of our people to prove it and make us remember". Thereafter, the events leading up to the pogrom are noted down in the chronicler's Book, each incident, every meeting of the leaders of the community, all conversations pertaining to safeguarding the memory of the town, are faithfully recorded: Moshe's first sermon is written down verbatim in the "Pinkas" and, receptive to every vibration, Shmuel concludes his entry with the sentence: "There was a long silence before the faithful dared look at one another". Shmuel did not only record words and silence but he scrupulously recorded the forced laughter of a congregant during the discussion of the fate of Kolvillág, as well as the pounding of his heart that "an obscure voice ordered him to record".

The conversation that takes place in the prison cell between Moshe and Shmuel, witnessed by Azriel, in many ways encapsulates their narrative viewpoints and prepares the reader for *The Oath* of silence in Moshe's sermon. Moshe argues that he has ceased to believe in the written word, in spite of his previous teachings to his disciple, young Azriel, that "nothing in Jewish history is unconnected", that everything is linked, from the sacrifice of Isaac and the destruction of the Temple to the Ukranian and Polish pogroms. He claims that the words uttered by Moses at Sinai have become distorted and exploited, and it is only the silence transmitted among the initiated "like a secret tradition" that eludes language. Shmuel's argument on the other hand is unequivocal: "A deed transmitted is a victory snatched from death. A witness who refuses to testify is a false witness". He reminds Moshe of the prominent role of the witness in Jewish tradition and his own sacred task of consigning everything to paper without daring to falsify testimony or distort the truth, even at the risk of antagonising those who do not want their words or deeds documented. He tells Moshe that it is his duty to record everything, "Even that which is beyond understanding", and explains that if Moshe refuses to answer a question: "I will write down that you could not or would not answer". Recalling this conversation, Azriel could not help smiling at the naiveté of his father, the historian, who would never have guessed then that his labour would be in vain and that his testimony would be forbidden.

After the dialogue that is never concluded and would not be resolved for fifty years, Shmuel steeps himself in martyrology as if to prove that the power of the written word would redeem the community and negate Moshe's anti-prophetic commandment. He studies names, dates, numbers, sources, motives and consequences. All the accounts of the martyrs of the pogroms follow and resemble one another and Shmuel realises that the name of Kolvillág will be added to the list. This again bears out Roskies' proposition that for the Jew, history conspired with literature to repeat the old archetypes over and over again. He states: "After all a pogrom was a pogrom. . .". Thematic formulas and details are applicable anywhere and only the place-names and dates would be changed.

Throughout Part 3 of the novel there are excerpts from the "Pinkas" describing the martyrs of pogroms dating back to the year 1193. They are situated in the narrative in such a way that they intrude on the narration of the present events establishing a continuity of suffering and death throughout the ages. The authenticating narrative device of Shmuel reading the extracts to his son, serves to link the historical events and characters of the ancient pogroms to the shadowy figures of catastrophe in the twentieth century. The last question Azriel asks his father on the eve of the onslaught is, who will write the ending of the "Pinkas?" His father answers: "The ending will not be given". But the chronicler hands over the Book to his son, telling him he will know what to say and what not to say, recalling Moshe's words earlier in the text about Rabbi Levi Yitzhak's belief that: "Man is responsible not only for what he says, but also for what he does not say".

The need to bear witness for the survivors of catastrophe seems most often related to the very reason they have been spared. Ezrahi, remarking on the testimonial imperative states: "The survivor, often the only one of his family or community to remain alive, almost invariably prefaced his account with a formulaic assertion of his vocation as a survivor: 'And I only am escaped alone to tell thee '". She cites an example of a fragment which has survived from the Hebrew Lamentation literature of the fourteenth century, written by the only survivor of a pogrom that had wiped out every inhabitant and destroyed all the holy books, except one Bible. This man, referring to himself as "the last ember," wrote a brief account of the destruction of the town on the pages of the one remaining Bible. This sense of urgency, intensified by the passage of time and the tenuousness of survival, gives credence to Azriel's testimonial imperative and the predominance of first-person narration. Azriel is the last and only survivor and witness "to have breathed the fiery, stifling air of Kolvillág". His fictional silence of fifty years may also be a reminder of the silence in the decades following the first frenzied memoirs and accounts of survivors of concentration camp experience. However, the need to bear witness is not the only motivating force behind his decision to tell the story. His primary reason is to save the life of the young man who is on the verge of committing suicide.

The thematic dialectic between life and death, and testimony and silence in *The Oath*, could not be realised without taking into account the narrative process which illuminates the way in which the tale is told and by whom it is told. Furthermore, it is the interaction of narrative voices that determine the structure of the novel. It must be remembered that Azriel is not the only narrator of the forbidden story. The paradoxical illusion that he does not break the oath of silence while the tale is being told is achieved by having several narrators share the responsibility of the narration. In a first-person narrative situation, the reader's centre of orientation lies in the fictional world as recorded or interpreted by the narrator who is telling the story. The questions arise whether the narrator's point of view is maintained throughout the narration and how the narrator is able to produce long dialogues, and monologues within dialogues, as direct quotations when such a feat of memory is beyond the capabilities of the first person narrator. But the narration of the story of *The Oath* transcends Azriel's viewpoint so that the reader does not depend on Azriel as the only voice for its transmission. The authorial narrator must be taken into account, even though after the first section of the book, the third person narration is sporadic, only being discerned through brief shifts in tense and occasional changes from the first-person "I" to the third-person "the old man." Moreover, these changes often occur in the same paragraph without a change of focus. While the reader cannot rely on another version of the story from the omniscient narrator, the story is told from three other viewpoints. Thus, the reader's centre of orientation shifts between the interwoven narrations of Azriel, Moshe and Shmuel. Each narrator is permitted to speak in his own voice, in his own way and in different contexts. Paradoxically, the oath of silence is sustained even though the story is finally told.

From the beginning of the novel the reader is under the impression that the voice of Azriel is divided. When Azriel encounters the young man for the first time and is asked who he is, he does not reply out loud, but answers silently: "Who am I? Azriel? Who am I? Moshe?", suggesting that their lives, voices and destinies are inexorably intertwined and interchangeable. Each time Azriel considers breaking the oath of silence, he evokes the name of his mad friend: "Moshe is not dead, I am. So go ahead, Moshe. Speak to us ... You speak, since you have sworn me to silence". On another occasion, when Azriel attempts to tell the young man about the town's most famous, respected and mysterious madman, he interrupts himself by saying that Moshe is the principal character of this tale and it is his story that deserves to be told. Repeatedly, Azriel claims that he cannot, nor does he have the right to give that which is not his. By evoking the narrative voice of Moshe to be the narrator of the forbidden story, Moshe shares the liability of its telling with his disciple.

In the same way as Azriel cannot tell of the vision of madness in Kolvillág without Moshe, so the tale cannot be told without the words carved by his father in the "Pinkas." The testimony of his father is also the testimony to his father. Shmuel's existence is bound up with the life of the community contained in the Book. He is not portrayed as a father figure but is totally identified with the town: "Whatever happens to the community I want to happen to myself as well". When the young man asks to see the diary, "the thick bound notebook, the old fashioned kind" that looks like a ledger, Azriel tears it from his hands and clasping it to his chest, reverses roles, "behaving like a father with his child". Yet Azriel reads from the blackened pages and recalls familiar anecdotes with his young listener who admits: "In one night he had me adopted by his entire community. So much so that I could find my way in his town". Just as Shmuel initiates Azriel into the tradition of the Book, so Azriel passes on to the young man the sacredness and value accorded to the written word. Each time the "Pinkas" is opened and the words are read, it is Shmuel who is speaking from the pages and in this way Azriel does not violate the oath of silence.

The short epilogue in *The Oath*, presented in italics, is the key to the interrelationship of the narrators. The young man, having received the story assumes the role of the new narrator. His first thought is that "Tomorrow is named Azriel." He is the link not only between the past, present and future but between the narrators. He, as the surrogate son and disciple of Azriel, is now in a similar position to that of the young Azriel in Kolvillág, who having inherited the unfinished story from the Book, is doomed to survival by his father. Similarly, the young man, having received the story, no longer has the right to die. He will retell it, bearing testimony to Azriel's oath, the written word of Shmuel and the silence of Moshe. Ironically, the last question he asks the old man is, "Who is Moshe?" Azriel answers: "You. I." And, half mockingly he adds, "You, when you open your eyes; I when I close mine." The last paragraph of the book is narrated by the omniscient narrator and while it serves to complete the circular process of the narrative, ensuring its continuity by the promise of its retelling, the reader is faced with a new puzzle:

> Then the young man obediently returned home, and so did the old man. That undoubtedly explains why they never saw each other again: Azriel had returned to die in my stead, in Kolvillág. (283)

The question is who will die in Azriel's stead in Kolvillág? Can the interchangeability of narrators be such that "my" refers to the young man?

The Oath is filled with questions, many of which are unanswerable. The conclusion remains open-ended forcing the reader to return to the novel's enigmatic beginning of denial and the old man's refusal to tell the story. Wiesel succeeds in creating the doubts and uncertainties about telling a forbidden story and sustains the secret silence surrounding it. Each of his narrators contribute to the communication of silence which is at the core of the novel. Moshe the Madman, is the author's advocate for a path as yet unexplored and untried – testimony without words. Shmuel's voice is the voice out of silence demanding to be heard in order to preserve the memory of the dead. Azriel, the silent survivor, is torn between his oath not to reveal the massacre of a whole community and his desire to save the life of one man. The young man represents Wiesel's listener who must inevitably become the new narrator forging a link between the memory of survivors of the Holocaust and the memory of a twentieth-century pogrom which is now his legacy and purpose for living. *The Oath* is a fictional work that allows a response to Jewish catastrophe on a continuum by using traditional archetypes, and, at the same time, through the interaction of its narrators, permits their testimony, as an act of commemoration, to be heard within varying levels of silence.

CHAPTER 7
CONCLUSION:
THE MUTE NARRATOR IN *THE TESTAMENT*

The paradoxical intention of entrusting a mute narrator to be the bearer of the tale is fully realised in *The Testament*. As this novel is the last one I will be dealing with in this study, I will attempt to show how the narrative strategies in this work are a culmination of Wiesel's previous fictional techniques. I will briefly draw on the novels following the trilogy to illuminate the recurring pattern of the silent narrators and the listeners.

As in all Wiesel's fiction, *The Testament* invites several possibilities of interpretation from the varying perpectives of its narrators. However, in this novel, for the first time, Wiesel clearly defines the function of his central narrator,

Paltiel Kossover, and develops him as the fictional hero of the story, tracing his life from birth to his execution in a prison cell in Krasnograd. His biography is specifically located in time and place and is based on historical and socio-political events in Europe and Soviet Russia before and after the Second World War. As the thrust of the novel is directed to the written testament of Kossover, which comprises most of the book, the reader is inevitably drawn to his version of the story, authenticated by history, in preference to the other narrators, who, by fragmenting the sequence of the narrative do not appear to have the same authoritative appeal. While in many respects this work, because of its articulate protagonist, is less demanding of its readers than the other novels, Wiesel is at the same time using the narrative strategy of the mute narrator who is ultimately responsible for retelling the tale.

The Testament has been described by Rosenfeld in "The Need to Transmit," as "a novel devoted to commemorating the tragedy that overtook Jewish cultural life in Soviet Russia". The historical background of the novel is certainly authentic and invites a reading of it on the level of history. Moreover, in 1965 Wiesel visited five cities in Russia and wrote a personal report on Soviet Jewry (originally intended as a series of articles), and later published in book form under the title *The Jews of Silence*. While Paltiel Kossover is a fictional character in *The Testament*, he is representative of some 30 Jewish writers who were executed on August 12, 1952 in the Soviet Union, their crime being "nothing more or less than that they were Yiddish writers, and as such were judged guilty of 'nationalism' or 'cosmopolitanism' and hence condemned as enemies of the Soviet state." As Rosenfeld goes on to explain: "Hundreds more – poets, novelists, essayists, editors, actors, artists, and musicians – preceded or were soon to follow them into death, victims of the Stalinist liquidation of Russian Jewish culture". Furthermore, after the revolution in Soviet Russia, and the defeat of Nazism, Jewish intellectuals believed for a while that it was possible to live as both Communist and Jew, upholding the beliefs of the Soviet state as well as contributing to Jewish cultural survival. The dialectic between Communism and Judaism is an important thematic consideration of the novel and structures the dramatic action of Kossover's story.

The title of the novel is also the title of the book within the novel, "The Testament of Paltiel Kossover," which is divided into nine clearly demarcated sections corresponding to various stages in the poet's life. The "book" is a written confession commissioned by Kossover's interrogator, the Citizen Magistrate, to whom most of his story is addressed. In part 1 of his "Testament" Kossover expresses his gratitude to his interrogator for allowing him to continue to exercise his profession in prison, and as a gesture of appreciation, admits his guilt to all charges, with the exception of those implicating others. He introduces himself by name to the magistrate who obviously is fully aware of his identity, having interrogated him "a thousand times on the crimes" for which he stands accused. Kossover, not only furnishes the magistrate with exact details of the date and place of his birth but offers him personal memories of his Talmudic teacher, and describes the pogrom perpetrated in his home town of Barassy. The reader becomes aware that the "Testament" of Kossover, while deliberately being directed to Citizen Magistrate, is written for a wider audience.

Part 2 of "The Testament" is a continuation of the first-person narrator's recollection of his family's traumatic move from Barassy, later known as Krasnograd, to Liyanov, a small town on the Romanian border. He recalls the celebration of his Bar Mitzvah, the speech he delivers to the congregants, as well "the most exalting" phase of his life in the House of Study after he is chosen to be the disciple of Reb Mendel-the-Taciturn. His meeting with Ephraim, for whom a glorious career as a rabbinic judge is predicted, proves to be the turning point in young Kossover's life. Slowly and systematically Ephraim instills in his friend the concepts of Communism which "allows man to overcome oppression and inequality swiftly". In Part 3 he takes leave of his Talmudic studies; his traditional Hasidic upbringing and his family to join Ephraim in his pursuit of the ideals of the Revolution.

The episodic narration of his journeys and adventures as a poet and an ardent Communist in Berlin, Paris, Palestine and Spain, where he fights as a soldier in the Spanish War of Liberation, spans the period from 1928 until his return to Russia shortly before the outbreak of war against Nazi Germany. This decade reflects the loves, hopes and beliefs of the protagonist and enables the reader to gain insight into his personality and the motivation behind his involvement in the ideals of Communism, which reflect his dilemma of rejecting his traditional religious upbringing. Ironically, his testament, which purports to be a confession, furnishes personal details of his life in Europe but does not contain any relevant information on his alleged "crimes" against the Soviet Union. Many of the people he names, who may be of interest to his interrogator, are the victims of purges or have already been liquidated or imprisoned by the NKVD. Similarly, in part 8 of his confession, he writes about his decision to settle in Soviet Russia and the "miraculous" intervention of the war which saves him from imprisonment, and allows him to serve the Red Army as a stretcher bearer. In the last "chapter" of

"*The Testament* of Paltiel Kossover," he informs the Citizen Magistrate of his hospitalisation in Lublin after being seriously wounded in the war, his meeting with Raissa who becomes his wife, and his decision to finally join the Communist Party. The publication of his collected poems, "I Saw My Father in a Dream," the birth of their son, Grisha, and the events leading to his arrest and imprisonment are narrated hurriedly as though he is aware that this would be the final installment of his testament. At no time, however, does he realise that the prison where he is being tortured, interrogated and is finally executed is in the town of his birth, and that his life story has ended where it began.

This brief outline of the substance of Kossover's testament is intended to show that the narrative situation of the narrator when telling his story conforms to a typical epic situation in fiction. As Bertil Romberg points out in *Studies on the Narrative Technique of the First Person Novel*, the most common epic situation is the fictitious memoir, where the narrator depicts his own life: "From his epic situation the narrator sees the events in retrospect . . . . He can present the full range of experiences in quite as sovereign a manner as the omniscient author". Moreover, he can point forward to coming events in the course of his narration for the benefit of the reader or to heighten tension. The natural dualism in the figure of the narrator is brought about because, as Romberg points out, "he both narrates and experiences, he is both old and young." of all Wiesel's fiction, it is the self-contained "book" within *The Testament* that can best be applied to the epic situation that "necessitates the work of a narrator sitting at his writing desk". In this case, Kossover's desk is a table in a prison cell where he is writing his memoir.

Unlike Wiesel's other narrators, Kossover believes that it

is possible to die of silence, "as one dies of pain, of sorrow, of hunger, of fatigue, of illness or of love". After his period of solitary confinement in the prison's "isolator", where there is a complete absence of sound, even from the guards who glide noiselessly past the cells "in special slippers," and give their orders in sign language, Kossover realises that "silence was a more sophisticated, more brutal torture than any interrogation session":

> [Silence] acts on the soul and fills it with night and death
> .... [I]t is not words that kill, it is silence. It kills impulse and passion, it kills desire and the memory of desire. It invades, dominates and reduces man to slavery. And once a slave of silence, you are no longer a man. (209)

A completely different dimension of silence is conveyed in *A Town Beyond the Wall*, when Michael says, "It's when I'm silent that I live; in silence I define myself". Michael endures his torture in prison because "silence was not an emptiness but a presence," which he could fill with memories of his past and re-enact dialogues with his friend, Pedro, who helped him discover the texture of silence.

However, it is not only in prison that Kossover discovers that silence could be "nefarious, evil, that it could drive man to lies, to treason". As a child he remembers the density and pressure of silence before the pogrom in Barassy that is "a source and harbourer of hostility and danger" preventing him from "breathing, from living". And yet it is that silence imposed by his father that miraculously saves his family from the massacre. Kossover's paradoxical experience of silence before the pogrom, which is declared a miracle by one of the Talmudic students who believes that God's intervention has made them mute, is not shared by Azriel, one of the narrators in *The Oath*. He describes the silence within silence at midnight before the onslaught in Kolvillág when, "The Angel of Death chooses its prey and proclaims mourning". The enemy is the sound of the silent midnight wreaking destruction on the town and its Jewish inhabitants, leaving only one survivor, whose testimony is sworn to silence.

When Kossover is nineteen and living in Berlin he begins writing poetry in order to express himself, and say what he thinks and feels about people, "not for the industrial tycoons with their pompous, sinister manners, but for their pitiful slaves, the wretches like myself". His friendship with Bernard Hauptman, an eloquent speaker and polemicist, as well as his love affair with Inge, Hauptman's former girlfriend, influence the young Talmudist's views on silence when he becomes an active supporter of the Communist Party. At a political meeting, Inge commands Kossover to shout loudly, to yell, to "make some noise," reprimanding his silence by saying: "To keep quiet is an act of sabotage". He continues writing poetry and newspaper articles, and enjoys attending public meetings, where speakers "preach, lecture, teach, thunder, vociferate, condemn and make demands depending on the slogans of the day". In Paris, when several of his poems and a short story are published by a newspaper, the editor adds a note of introduction for his readers: "Paltiel Kossover, Jewish by birth and poet by profession, had abandoned the God of his ancestors for the working class, the superannuated Torah for the Communist ideal, idle contemplation for the class struggle..." This opinion does not disturb Kossover, nor is he concerned with the mediocrity of his early poetry: "What was important for me was to be published".

A reader of Kossover's first poems is a "mysterious

messenger" called David Aboulesia, who, in his endless search for the Messiah, appears and disappears throughout Kossover's journey. On reading Kossover's poem, he sadly remarks that "a poet who doesn't look beyond the wall is like a bird without a song". He is the voice and the conscience of Kossover's traditional past, and reminds him of his former teacher Rebbe Mendel-the-Taciturn. Although Aboulesia is a madman and a wandering beggar, Wiesel does not develop him as a character or a narrator in the novel, and in fact uses him, at times, as a vehicle for his ironic humour. Aboulesia's fleeting presence remains shrouded in obscurity until the examining magistrate discovers his name in Kossover's "Testament." Each time his name is mentioned, the magistrate flies into a rage. This "incredible, impossible character" seems to appear unexpectedly, "in the weirdest, most outlandish places, be it in the market in Odessa or a brothel in Paris". The magistrate, convinced that Aboulesia is responsible for organizing an international network of spies and has accomplices inside the Kremlin walls, orders a search to be carried out by special agents. Although "never uncovering the slightest clue," this investigation goes on for months. The existence of this elusive stranger remains an enigma, not only for the narrator and his interrogator but ironically for the reader as well.

When in Spain, Kossover meets a man, who resembles David Aboulesia, bearing a message of reprimand, and reminding Kossover of his responsibility as a Jew: "It's the Communist who came here to shed his name and his past in order to become an international soldier". But, Kossover believes that he is fighting for "everything that stands for the honour of being a man". However, on his return to his deserted childhood home after the war, he feels the "dark mass of infinite, unspeakable, tumultuous sadness," which he can only contain in silence, and later expresses in a poem to his father. Kossover who regards words as his life considers himself to be the victim of his poetry. The last paragraph of his prison writings reflect not only the fear of not being heard or understood but express an optimism for the immortality of the word: "Tomorrow I shall go on writing the 'Testament of Paltiel Kossover,' filling it with details, turning it into a document of the times – in which the experiences of the past will serve as signs for the future". Kossover, at the end of his life, in many ways is the antithesis of Azriel in *The Oath*, for whom there is no tomorrow because the past can never serve as a sign for the future. For the old man, silence is more powerful than the word, "it draws its strength and secret from a savagely demented universe doomed by its wretched and deadly past".

It must be taken into account that while Kossover's testament constitutes the major part of the novel, and Kossover is both the author of the document as well as the central narrator of *The Testament*, Wiesel structures the novel in such a way that the other narrators who fragment the story provide the essence of its meaning. Before the novel begins, the author, Elie Wiesel, inserts a short introduction authenticating the existence of Grisha Paltielovich Kossover who arrived at Lod airport in Israel in July 1972. After making a few cursory enquiries from an official, he discovers that the young man is Paltiel Kossover's son, that he comes from Krasnograd, and that he is mute. The author realises that the poet was executed at the same NKVD dungeons in Krasnograd as the more illustrious writers of that period. Although Kossover was a lesser known poet than well known figures such as Peretz Markish and Dovid Bergelson, the author nevertheless admits that he admires his only published work, "I Saw

My Father in a Dream." Furthermore, he maintains that he was responsible for having had eight of his poems translated into three languages. He invites the boy to stay with him in his apartment in Jerusalem, thinking of the arduous task ahead of him, "getting his mute son to talk". This introduction, both casual and conversational, has the impact of immediacy on the reader, particularly as it is signed by the initials of the author, "E.W.". The authority of his concealed presence in the subsequent narration imposes a reality not only on the events of the story, but also on the narrators themselves. Towards the end of the novel, the author makes one further *in persona* appearance, when he informs Grisha that his mother will not be arriving in Israel.

Wiesel uses several other authenticating narrative devices before the novel begins. He inserts a letter written by Kossover to his son, Grisha, whom he had not seen since he was an infant, in which Kossover doubts whether the boy will receive the letter, and whether the contents of his "Testament" will be transmitted. He attempts to explain to his son that his poems are neither a spiritual nor a poetic biography, "they're simply songs offered to my father, whom I had seen in a dream". He informs him that he has pleaded guilty, not to the charge that has no meaning for him, but for not having lived as his father did. He ironically states: "I lived as a Communist and I die as a Jew". The letter, written just before Kossover's death, is a personal and emotional legacy of a father to his son, and is offered as a separate document which permits the reader the privilege of sharing it with Grisha.

In addition to the letter, Wiesel includes a map of the pre-World War 2 frontiers of Europe and Russia, to enable the reader to follow the "Travels of Paltiel Kossover." Whereas in *The Oath*, the young man pours over maps in a

CONCLUSION: THE MUTE NARRATOR IN *THE TESTAMENT* 149

futile search for the town of Kolvillág, the reader of *The Testament* is able to trace each destination of Kossover's journey, verifying the authority of the narrator and his story. A third authenticating narrative strategy Wiesel employs is the inclusion of several of Kossover's published and unpublished poems. Under each poem Wiesel inserts in parenthesis the phrase, "Translated from the Yiddish," which gives an added veracity to Kossover's profession as a poet, albeit a second-rate poet.

However, it is the omniscient narrator who sets the opening scene of the novel and introduces the reader to Grisha who is reading and re-reading his father's "Testament." In the first paragraph of the book, the name of Victor Zupanev is mentioned, "the man who could not laugh – who passes on to him the story of the story of the Jewish poet slain far away". While Zupanev appears only in the imagination and memory of Grisha, who continually hears his hoarse staccato voice, he is the invisible narrator who orchestrates the narration of the entire novel. Although the narrative structure of the novel is dependent upon and unified by the third-person narrator, the reader is constantly alerted to the crucial role of Zupanev who is telling the story to Grisha, his only listener. As the teller of the tale, it is incumbent upon Zupanev to transform his listener into the narrator, despite Grisha's muteness.

The authorial narrator moves back and forth in time and place, changing tenses and continually shifting the focus of the story. He is able to report on events in Jerusalem, visualise Kossover's dream moments before his arrest by the Secret Police, imagine Grisha's early childhood in Krasnograd, interpret Raissa's thoughts and feelings, and reproduce dialogues between the characters in the book. The past and present merge in the telling of the tale, and the reader is forced to abandon the boundaries of time and space. The narrator, for instance, begins a sequence of events in Jerusalem on the night before the expected arrival of Grisha's mother from Vienna, continues with a vivid scene from Grisha's youth, interposes a monologue of Kossover in the first-person, and returns to the immediate present of Grisha's relationship with Katya, a young widow, who lives across the street. He then reverts back to his interpretative role of omniscience remarking that Paltiel Kossover in writing his "Testament," sought precision: "Every word contains a hidden meaning; every sentence sums up a wide range of experiences." Almost as an afterthought, he adds that Kossover hints at this somewhere in the document, "Page . . . which page? . . . There on page 43, at the bottom". Not only does the narrator continually reinforce Kossover's status as the author of the book but he firmly establishes his own illusion of credibility.

At times the third-person narrator acts as the narrative voice of the speechless youth who would have liked to have been the narrator of his father's "broken life and his hidden death": "Your son, your heir, can articulate only unintelligible sounds; your only son is mute" . And yet, when Grisha meets Katya, who is mute in her own way, never talking of her husband killed in the war, he realises that he is unable to tell her of his own life, his father's work, his feelings for his mother, or Zupanev, the old watchman of ghosts: "Even if he were not mute he would have remained silent" . The only time Grisha breaks his silence in the novel is when his friend Zupanev asks him how he became mute.

The story Grisha writes in a notebook given to him by Zupanev is yet another narrative device Wiesel uses for verifying his tale. Not only does it serve as an alternative narrative view point but it prefigures Grisha's role as the narrator of his father's testament. Zupanev, aware of the reversal of roles he wishes to impose on the boy, tells Grisha that he will keep the notebook "together with those of your father". Grisha writes his story briefly, almost dispassionately, in short concise sentences as though to measure each word against the silence that engulfs him. He begins by making a short statement about Dr Mozliak, his mother's lover, whom he suspects of working for the Security police, and admits, without remorse, that he hates him. Grisha realises that the physician's frequent visits to their apartment while his mother is ill, are for the purpose of interrogating him about his father. At first he withdraws into absolute silence, but Dr Mosliak is a "specialist" and "extracted words from me, sentences, shreds of silence. The more I spoke, the less I existed; he robbed me of what I cherished most". Suddenly, one day, "the miracle occurred": "overcome by rage, an uncontrollable spasm made me close my jaws over my tongue. I cut it in two. I lost consciousness and from then on I have been incapable of pronouncing a word".

Grisha concludes his story by telling Zupanev that had he not been mute, their paths would not have crossed and, "I would have known nothing but silence and ashes". The gravity of his desperate action is conveyed to the reader through the immediacy of Grisha's narration of the story in his own words rather than through the third-person narrator. Grisha uses language in such a way as to transmit his speechless world. In *The Gates of the Forest*, this experience is reversed after Gregor gives up speech to play the role of the mute in the village where he is being hidden. It is under extreme provocation that he breaks his silence to declare that he is a Jew. Grisha, on the other hand, in order not to betray his father whose existence is inextricably linked with his own, destroys his faculty of speech to become a mute. But, ironically, because he is mute, Victor Zupanev is able to tell him the story of his father's life and arranges his escape from Russia.

Zupanev is the embodiment of all Wiesel's elusive narrators in his fiction. He is a listener who has been transformed by the act of listening into a teller of tales. He is a messenger from the dead to the living, a teacher who transmits his knowledge gained from silence. He is ageless with no distinguishing physical characteristics. His face is so expressionless, and his features are so "monotonous" that the only appropriate description of him would be "anonymity". He is like Azriel in *The Oath*, whose physical features no one could recall: "Some spoke of his round, puffy face while others described it as angular and expressive". He has the enigmatic quality of Gavriel in *The Gates of the Forest*, who is either mad or exceptionally intelligent. Whether Gavriel's stories are intended to teach a lesson, convey a recollection, transmit a message or "make some dangerous and terrible confession", is never made apparent to the listener because he has "a thousand voices." The description Zupanev gives of himself to Grisha, is however, more explicitly stated than in the other novels where the identity of the narrator often remains unknown. He admits that no one ever looks at him as he blends into the landscape: "I don't attract attention. I'm a human chameleon . . . Everything about me is so ordinary that people look at me without seeing me." But he sees them: "After all, a watchman's duty is to watch". However, before becoming a watchman in Krasnograd, Zupanev was a stenographer in the prison court during the interrogation of Paltiel Kossover.

It is the quality of invisibility that enables Zupanev to learn the full story of Kossover's life. From his. corner in the court room, where he takes notes as a clerk, he is able

CONCLUSION: THE MUTE NARRATOR IN *THE TESTAMENT*

to observe the prosecutor, the magistrate, the colonel and the accused without being seen by them: "I was a piece of furniture. An instrument. Part of the scenery. The invisible man from whose attention nothing escaped". Zupanev, like Shmuel, the scribe of the "Pinkas" in *The Oath*, transcribes everything he sees and hears, "at first for them, later for your father." He records "the hunger pangs, the agonies of thirst, the wounds of memory" and even describes the test of silence which Kossover manages to overcome. As the interrogation drags on, Zupanev notes that Kossover's case was unique in the annals of the court. The entire apparatus of the NKVD is placed in jeopardy. Zupanev, having been conditioned by his profession, assures his listener that he does not wish to exaggerate or embroider upon the prisoner's resistance to interrogation, and he writes down only the facts "as in a police report." Yet, when he tells Grisha how his father is finally manipulated by the magistrate, who discovers Kossover's weakness, he can no longer play the part of the dispassionate court reporter. He admits: "My idol became a puppet. The writer in him succumbed to the temptations of writing, to the mysterious spell of the word". But, just as the poet relents to the project of writing the story of his life, so Zupanev, through reading "*The Testament*," is transformed from the invisible scribe to Kossover's messenger. He has learned to understand how "one can live with words alone". He discovers how to ask questions, and through his writings Kossover teaches Zupanev how to care.

This element of change brought about in the listener through having heard the tale is crucial to an understanding of the role of the narrator in Wiesel's fiction, and is the key to Zupanev's pivotal role in *The Testament*. In spite of his being a minor character in the novel, it is from Zupanev's point of view that the narrative process of the novel is revealed. Kossover's "Testament" is the tale that Zupanev retells to his mute son. While his infrequent and sporadic appearances, contained in the italicised sections of the novel, intrude into the first-person narration of Kossover's story and often obscure the point of view of the omniscient narrator, they provide the meaning for the strange relationship that develops between Zupanev and Grisha, the teller and the listener.

Towards the beginning of the novel, Zupanev introduces himself by saying, "I have never laughed in my life" and asks his listener whether he has met anyone else who is incapable of laughter. This inability to laugh differentiates him from all Wiesel's other fictional narrators. As laughter is such an important theme and is used as a narrative device in the place of language, particularly in *The Gates of the Forest*, where Gavriel's laughter echoes throughout the narrative, Wiesel is offering a new and different dimension to "the extraordinary old man" who bears witness. Each time he appears (which is clearly demarcated in italics to emphasise the difference between his narrative voice and the voices of the other narrators), he mentions this unique disability. The change that occurs when Zupanev learns to laugh does not in any way affect the resolution of the central story, but it is the determining factor in the narrative process, influencing the way in which the tale is retold. Zupanev explains to Grisha that his parents, neighbours, adversaries, doctors, and even his teachers tried to make him laugh through various means, even depriving him of food, water and sleep. Nor did the "fortune tellers, showmen, monks, scoundrels, witches, acrobats, clowns, fakirs" have any success. And because he did not know how to laugh, he had "no real friends, no real enemies, no mistresses, no illegitimate children – I had no one, I was no one". But then, "a poet, different from the others, a crazy Jew, burst into my life and changed it by telling me about his own".

In retelling the tale Zupanev adds a new dimension to *The Testament*, not only by supplementing it with events of Kossover's life during his imprisonment, but through telling Grisha stories of his own. As a watchman, he is aware of the private lives of the people in Krasnograd, and takes a particular interest in Grisha's family. He knows about "prisons and torture sessions, judges and clowns" and even has access "to the forbidden memories of an entire people reduced to silence". As a storyteller he has the qualities of Wiesel's beggars, madmen and messengers who weave fantastic stories from the past to bring them into the present, or tell stories of the present as though they are legends. He speaks of others to avoid speaking of himself: "A whole procession of men, well known and obscure, ordinary and odd, peopled his stories". As a teacher, he explains to Grisha the events of the day, Russian politics, the problems of emigration to Israel, episodes of Jewish history and the rudiments of Yiddish. He recounts stories that Grisha does not know "and should know".

When Zupanev first meets Grisha he tells him that he has learned "to hear the words people leave unsaid, to read the words one promises oneself never to utter". Like Rabbi Zusia in *The Oath*, who commands Azriel to speak without words, so the old watchman persuades his mute listener to "make believe" that he is speaking and he will be heard. One of the stories he tells Grisha concerns the enforced silence of an historian, Hersh Talner, incarcerated in prison. One night, through some "miracle," the historian is given a pencil stub and a single sheet of white paper. Conscious of his mission, his memory overloaded with facts and images, the prisoner realises the torturous task of conveying "the haunted faces and broken bodies, the confessions and denials, the testimony of the dead and the appeals of the dying" without mutilating their memory. When dawn breaks, he has not yet written a single sentence, but Hersh Talner's red hair had turned completely white. Zupanev, in explaining the significance of this story to Grisha, says that it is not only the crazy historians who will bear witness, but it is the mute orators: "the mute poets will cry forth our truth".

Zupanev's life and the way in which he narrates his stories carry the meaning of silence in the novel. In choosing Grisha to be the recipient of his tale, Zupanev is ensuring the silence needed not only to preserve the memory of the dead poet and the death of the Jews but for survival without words. Moreover, he is entrusting his role as narrator to his mute listener who will, in turn, become the new teller of the tale. Before his departure for Israel, Grisha memorises every page and verse of his father's "Testament." As the watchman reads in his low, monotonous voice from the notebooks, he is aware that:

> Grisha was listening, committing every sentence, every comma to his memory, disciplining his mind, motionless, his lips half open, tensed to the breaking point. He listened, he listened gravely, intensely, barely breathing. Only his eyes mirrored life; he listened with his eyes, he listened, registering every word, every nuance, every hesitation. He owed it to himself to remember it all, to store it all, to let nothing slip by. Nobody listened the way he did; no other memory was equal to his. (301)

Zupanev acknowledges how fortunate it is that Grisha is mute. He says: "They are letting you go. They do not suspect the power of a mute." Nor, in fact, did the authorities suspect the power of Zupanev, because for them a stenographer is "just barely a living object".

The final section of *The Testament* belongs to Zupanev's narration, in which he describes the last night of Kossover's life and how he witnessed the execution, carried out before dawn in Kossover's cell. The order had come from Stalin, and the examining magistrate, annoyed and frustrated that he could not bring the trial to its proper conclusion, gives Zupanev permission to be present at the execution. The idea occurs to the stenographer that he would like to reassure Kossover that his writings are being well protected, but he realises it would be cruel to warn the poet he is about to die. He also has a desire to ask Kossover whether he as ever really laughed: "either you don't speak of it because you have never laughed, or because you have laughed so much that it does not occur to you to mention it". But Zupanev keeps his silence, which is shattered by Kossover's unfinished sentence before he is shot: "You must understand, the language of a people is its memory, and its memory ...." . Zupanev, the invisible witness to their "filthy business", tells Grisha that "on the day your father's song will come to haunt them from all corners of the globe", he will laugh at last , "for all the years I tried so hard to laugh and did not succeed". With the death of Kossover, Zupanev experiences a strange sensation: "My heart is broken but I know that I shall laugh". He suddenly understands that the dead poets will force men like himself to laugh, and that is why he says: "I implant in you his memory and mine, I must, my boy, you understand, I must. Otherwise ...". The book ends with a sentence that has just begun. The ellipsis promises continuity: the new narrator will retell the tale.

This reversal of roles between the listener and the teller is essential to the narrative process in Wiesel's fiction, particularly after the trilogy. The change that occurs carries with it the silence that is integral to the act of listening, and has a crucial bearing on the way in which the tale is narrated. In *The Gates of the Forest* the first part of the novel is devoted to the relationship between Gregor and Gavriel in the forest, where Gregor is the listener to Gavriel's stories. When Gavriel disappears Gregor, continually haunted by his absence, becomes his messenger and retells his tales. Michael, the narrator in *The Town Beyond the Wall*, relives his past in order to endure his present torture in prison and imaginatively interchanges his own life and stories with his friend Pedro, who is both listener and teller. *A Beggar in Jerusalem* is filled with storytellers and listeners but it is David, the central narrator, who is forced to exchange roles with Katriel after he vanishes in the war and is the one to bear witness for him. The narrative strategy in *The Oath* is more explicitly realised than in Wiesel's previous novels. The old man, Azriel, breaks his oath of silence to tell the tale of Kolvillág to his young listener who must retell the story. Each of these novels, in its own way, through the narrative process, expresses different dimensions to the silence of the narrator and the listener.

It is, however, in *The Testament* that the most convincing portrayal of the mute narrator is offered. Zupanev tells Grisha "Since they cannot make you talk, you shall be the ideal messenger just as I was. Nobody will suspect you, just as nobody suspected me". Although Grisha is literally mute and the reader cannot doubt the silence that will be transmitted through the retelling of the tale, this novel in many ways offers a conclusion to the central concern of this project: it is not only what Wiesel says but the way in which he says it that is of the greatest interest in his fiction.

Wiesel's stature as a novelist in the literature of testimony is accomplished through the creation of is own fictional universe in which he presents fragments of his individual vision in book after book. Through the narrative process the reader, like the listener of his tales, can share the idea Keats expressed: "of being in uncertainties, mysteries, doubts, without any irritable reaching after fact and reason".

APPENDIX: INTERVIEW

My conversation with Elie Wiesel took place in his New York apartment overlooking Central Park. His handshake was warm as he graciously welcomed me into his study where books, manuscripts and journals lined the walls from floor to ceiling. His quiet, melodious voice, his deeply lined face and modest manner reminded me of the charismatic effect he had on me during my first personal encounter with him in Johannesburg in 1975, when I was privileged to interview him for *The Jewish Times*. I explained that I had recently begun research for an academic thesis on the literary aspects of his novels. This is an adaptation of the tape recording of our conversation:

M.B: In *Dimensions of the Holocaust* you stated that there is no literature of the Holocaust, in that it is a contradiction in terms. You explain that one cannot write about a situation which goes beyond its very description: "a novel about Treblinka is either not a novel or not about Treblinka." You do, however, say there is a literature of testimony. Do you regard this as a new genre?

E.W:Yes. I think it is a new genre because the event is such an exceptional event. That is why silence plays such an important part in testimony. We have to invent a language, and that is always a philosophical problem.

M.B:I will return to the question of silence later, but at this point I would like to ask whether you think that the witnesses are the only ones who can write the literature of testimony?

E.W:As testimony, yes. There is a great controversy going on: who should write, who has the right to deal with the Holocaust? Only those who were there? Others can, and should, if there is enough respect in dealing with the question. Even then, it is not testimony. A poorly written book by a survivor is more important than an excellently written book by a great writer. As testimony, not as literature. In literature, of course, the writer is more important.

M.B:In his book, In Conversation with Elie Wiesel, Harry James Cargas, a leading Christian theologian, refers to your writing as belonging to the genre of Lazarene literature. Do you accept this term?

E.W:Francois Mauriac mentions that. He was the first to call it Lazarene literature. I do not like it. I do not like the Christian connotation applied to my work. He put it in his preface to *Night*. [Mauriac wrote that he was first drawn to the young Wiesel by "that look, as of Lazarus risen from the dead, yet still within the grim confines where he had strayed, stumbling among the shameful corpses".]

Mauriac went even further – he dedicated his book on Jesus, The Son of Man, to me, and said something like Elie Wiesel was a crucified Jewish child. I do not like this Christological vocabulary. I have my own. So I don't like the term Lazarene.

M.B:Why do think that so many non-Jewish scholars have not only written a great deal about you, but seem almost to have "adopted" you?

E.W:Perhaps they need someone.

M.B:Almost all your work – your novels, plays, poems, dialogues, essays and even the articles you write for newspapers and journals – is written in French and then translated into English. Do you feel that French, the language of adoption, helps to convey your message and is less of a betrayal than your mother-tongue?

E.W:I have dealt with this question in the Cargas book of Conversations. I explain it all there. Had I wanted to write in Hungarian I would have had an easier task but I didn't want to; I even tried to forget Hungarian. The Hungarian language reminded me too much of the Hungarian gendarmes and they were brutal . . . . It's easier to learn a new language than to forget an old one. I could have written in Hebrew or Yiddish. Why I chose French, I don't know; maybe it was because it was harder. I'm sure that symbolically it meant something to me: it meant a new home. The language became a haven, a new beginning, a new possibility, a new world. To start expressing myself in a new language was a defiance. The defiance became even stronger because the French language is Cartesian. Reason is more important than anything else. Clarity. French is such a non-mystical language. What I try to transmit with or through that language is mystical experience. So the challenge is greater.

M.B:Were you influenced by many French writers?

E.W:Yes, the modern writers. Camus and Malraux much more than the others. Mauriac, of course. That was a great period in French literature. But my real influence came from the Jewish writers and Jewish religious literature.

M.B:Are you satisfied that the translations of your work are a true reflection of your writing?

E.W:Some yes, some no. Some are better than others, unfortunately. It is very hard for an author to judge for himself. Some are written in English anyway. Four Hasidic Masters and Five Biblical Portraits are written in English. Furthermore, there are translations in other languages which I cannot judge: in Japanese, for instance. But, the English translations, at least the later translations, I am more or less satisfied with. I have collaborated on two – *A Beggar in Jerusalem* and *The Jews of Silence*. Since then my wife has done the translations. I would like some of the earlier ones redone. *Night* should be redone.

M.B:In my research I have found that the literary critics and commentators have dealt mainly with the themes and theological aspects of your work. I am particularly interested in the narrative strategies in your novels. Is your narrative style deliberately complex or is it a result of the ineffability of the Holocaust experience.

E.W:You know, it is very rarely I speak of my work. I do not know how to speak of it. Morally it is very difficult, but my books explain themselves. I write every book three times. The first time more easily, since the emphasis is on conversation. It is three quarters of the size. The idea is of course to obtain simplicity. And simplicity should be established. But some are very complicated, very complex, in fact.

M.B:Is this the reason why some of the critics interpret this narrative complexity as "lapses of voice," referring I think to your constant journeys into the past, into Hasidic tales and legends?

E.W:Perhaps that is so.

M.B:Do you think they prefer your first novel *Dawn* to some of your later fiction because of its compact style and the seeming simplicity of the story set in Palestine at the time of the British occupation? Or is it perhaps that in your more complex novels there is a refusal to recognise that the narrative technique is part of your message?

E.W:The technique comes later. The message has its own importance. And that is why the third version I write must be a subconscious version. The second time the book is already looking at itself.

M.B:You have used many literary modes in your writing and often what you say in your essays is not only different but contradictory in the context of your novels. Is it because your narrators can assert things in a work of fiction that you cannot say in an essay?

E.W:That is why I choose essays, poems, plays, novels and even commentaries on the Bible – I have covered everything. I did not want to leave anything out. I am even trying to invent a genre – the Dialogues. Anything that exists I want to try out.

M.B:In every work there is a Hasidic story. Is it your base of truth?

E.W:It is the nerve centre, but it is also the oeuvre I try to create.

The work of a writer is not simply the sound of his voice. I tried to create a universe, and to recreate a universe; to find a bearing, to find stories, a pattern. I have had all the opportunities from the writers in the world to say that two and two are five. It is my project as a writer, and I must keep to it. If I say on page 1 that two and two are five, then I must say it on page 6. I have to create my own pattern.

M.B:There is a kind of timelessness in your narratives. They move from the immediate present to the near past, to the historical past, to the legendary past. This shifting time scheme is often a problem for the reader.

E.W:... Except on the clock time; there it is always the same time. There are twenty-four hours; one day and one night. There are three laws of Aristotle; the unity of time is one of them. Of course, beyond that I like to move quickly from present to past in the tenses. Switching tenses is very important to create the time change.

M.B:The characters in your novels are never well defined or fully drawn. Is it because they are universal characters?

E.W:It is possible, because every character purports to be acknowledged as a character. This is simply because we are living at a time where we are so discreet, or should be discreet .... Nobody wants to feel himself or herself to be a character who is not like someone today.

M.B:In *The Oath* the old man tells the story of the devastation of the town of Kolvillág to a young man. This young listener has neither an age nor a name. Why is it that we know so little about him?

E.W:He is young and tragic. If he had a name he would not be that tragic.

M.B:Is naming very important?

E.W:In Jewish tradition, yes.

M.B:*The Gates of the Forest* is very much about names. The protaganist Gregor gives away his Hebrew name, Gavriel, to a stranger. After the war he searches everywhere for Gavriel in order to recover his name. If you do not have a name, do you still have an identity?

E.W:Identity, yes. Names are something else. Identity is the self; names are the past event of the self. After all, in our generation, the Jewish child actually bears the name of someone who died. So there is the same name after a few generations. And so we can have identity without names, but the names are that which culminates everything.

M.B:Some of your novels are not located in a particular place or even in a fictionalised setting. In *The Oath* for example, one critic maintains that the story was located in a modern metropolis. Would you agree with this interpretation?

E.W:It could be anywhere because it is really the whole world the problems, the despair . . .

M.B:In every novel, you seem to have at least one beautiful character, like Pedro in *The Town Beyond the Wall*.

E.W:Yes. Otherwise, if it is to create more ugliness, what for? *The Town Beyond the Wall* has been my favourite novel. I love it.

M.B: Why is it that the structural organisation of Town, which is divided into four parts of equal length, is so different from *The Oath*, with its uneven division into three sections?

E.W: I wanted to create diversity. In *The Town Beyond the Wall* there are four prayers; in *The Gates of the Forest* there are four seasons. In *A Beggar in Jerusalem* there is something else; it is like *Dawn* with all the complexities: there is a mixture, chapters upon chapters. *The Testament*, of course, is different. It is to find something new, not to stay in the same place.

M.B: In your fiction, the listeners and narrators seem to have interchangeable roles. Is it because once the listeners have heard the story, they become narrators in order to retell the tale?

E.W: You are very perceptive. It's true, because it is based on what I believe to be the foundation of storytelling: that anyone who listens becomes the narrator. As for testimony itself, it becomes a link among generations. So one generation talks, another listens. We are a listening tradition, and it is still based on the transmission of what we have heard.

M.B: The central theme of your work seems to be silence. But, the multidimensional perspectives created from the use of your various narrators to tell the tale, seem to convey silence not only as a theme, but as a narrative technique.

E.W: Perhaps that is so. Silence is one of the main themes.

M.B: In *The Oath*, one of your narrators says that for your silence to have meaning you must stay alive. There is a different kind of silence in *The Testament*. I think it is Kossover who says: "I didn't know that it was possible to die of silence". Are these paradoxical aspects of silence?

E.W:Silence is a universal silence. Just as there is time and space, there is silence, which means that there is life in silence and death in silence. There is torture in silence. Actually, it is an adaptation of silence. How do you find silence in silence?

M.B:There is still another variation of silence in *The Town Beyond the Wall*. Michael, the protagonist, says: "It is when I am silent that I define myself" -that I live. Are you saying that it is not only in life, but it is also in death?

E.W:Yes. You cannot live without water, you cannot live without silence.

M.B:And yet, in *The Oath*, you explore the narrator's dilemma of living with silence. In his sermon before the massacre, Moshe the Madman explains that there must always be one storyteller, one survivor, one witness. He says: "To forget constitutes a crime against memory, against justice: whoever forgets becomes the executioner's accomplice". He then proclaims that silence will be the new way: "We are going to impose the ultimate challenge, not by language but by the absence of language, not by the word but by the abdication of the word". He maintains furthermore, that the only possible solution is to testify no more. Is this another manifestation of silence as testimony?

E.W:It is a variation of silence. Silence should become another way. I am trying to go deeper into the same oath, the same word, the same approach, the same question.

M.B:After the old man breaks *The Oath* of silence by telling the story, will the young man have to bear the same silence throughout his lifetime?

E.W:There are two things to remember: one may do anything, one must do anything to save a life. Nothing is more sacred than saving life, even in the regions of death. The point is that once the narrator speaks, the other one must become the narrator. He is forcing him. And it is always in the context of Jewish tradition. We were forced to reveal it; we were condemned to accept it. Once we have accepted it, we are not free to resist. He did not really want to be in that state. He wanted to die. The purpose is not to have heard.

M.B:In that sense, is no survivor or witness free?

E.W:In no way. Survival imprisons. It tries to set up witnesses.

M.B:It seems that the reluctance of the narrators to tell the story is part of the dilemma. Is it because the true story is always an impossible one to tell, and that you are continually searching for other ways of telling it?

E.W:Of course.

M.B:I am intrigued with the narrative devices you use in your latest novel, *The Testament*. The preface is signed E. W.; the setting is at Lod airport on a particular afternoon when a group of Russian Jews arrive in Israel. There is the implication that the narrated events actually occurred. You present documentary evidence such as a letter, a map, a book of poems and *The Testament* of a prisoner incarcerated by the K.G.B.

E.W:They are creating the roots. It is done for that. In fact, in the French version, I did not sign the preface E. W. It was simply "The Author." But I wanted to make it even stronger in the English version. It is true I have followed this noma for some time already. There is not a person, but a character. So the problem is how do

you take something that did not happen and make it happen.
[At this point Wiesel showed me the French and English edition of *The Testament* and pointed out other significant differences. Only the English version of the novel contains a map which was suggested to him by his American publisher. The French version ends with a full stop, while the English version ends with: "Otherwise . . ."]

M.B:Your use of different kinds of dialogues in *The Testament* is an interesting narrative device. Why is the dialogue between Zupanev, the court stenographer, and Grisha, Paltiel Kossover's mute son, in italics?

E.W:It is another technique. It is also called the "universing of time."

M.B:On the other hand, the dialogue between Kossover and the Chief Magistrate is rooted in time and place. Is it possible that during the Stalinist regime, such a dialogue would have taken place between the accuser and the accused in the K.G.B.?

E.W:It is possible. It wasn't the Chief Magistrate, it was a Citizen Magistrate. They have their own system. They did not make judgement; they did not pass sentence. They are interrogators and usually they choose interrogators from people who know something. They can be psychologists, psychiatrists . . . They do create a universe. The question is not that it took place, but how do we know about it? I had problems, great problems. The funny part is that I admired two writers amongst those who were killed. One was a poet, the other was a novelist and a mystic. I actually tried to make Paltiel Kossover something like them. When the book came out in France, I gave a lecture at the University of Geneva. Someone came to me afterwards and said: "How did you know my father so well?" I asked him who he was, and he answered:

"Shimon Markish." And not only that: he corroborated all that I had felt intuitively, even that he had returned to religion in the last years... It's incredible! Even more than that: I asked how he knew his father was there? Had he gone back? Did he talk to his mother? Did he talk to his father? How could he think...? He said: "You see, they brought us there, in the K.G.B. office." I have just published an introduction to the poems of Peretz Markish and in it I tell the story of how I met Shimon Markish.[1]

M.B: In *The Testament* there are several poems written by your fictive poet Kossover. At the end of each poem is the phrase: "Translated from the Yiddish." Is this done to make them more authentic?

E.W. There was a tremendous response to the book in France. I have had letters from people who wanted the original copies of Kossover's poems and wanted to know where to find them. I fell in love with Paltiel Kossover. I was so much taken by him, I did not want to finish the book.

M.B: In the novel, you explore the motif of laughter, or rather the absence of laughter. Why is it that Zupanev cannot laugh?

E.W: It is really for narrative purposes. I needed to find a way out, to get this book out as testimony. Nobody can say why Zupanev cannot laugh, except possibly Zupanev. I wrote this book over 15 years, until I found a way. I did not know how to turn this project into a story. Once I had decided that the only person who survived all this prejudice was one who could not laugh, then why should he? At that point, the anecdote becomes part of the story. This means that I take it from one level and shift it to another. The importance of technique is that once it has been filled, I can turn to other considerations: my obsession with laughter.

M.B: And is it Zupanev who puts the whole thing together?

E.W: He is the one. He says in the beginning: "I can't laugh" and he sees the whole thing, only because he can't laugh.

M.B. Is it perhaps his glimpse of madness?

E.W: Oh, he cannot laugh because he sees too much. He sees the weakness of man. He writes. He is a stenographer in the K.G.B. He sees the change in man. You asked a very fine question. It goes back to the idea that I try to expose: that one person can change everything.

M.B: The idea that the listener, the mute, Kossover's son, is going to be the new narrator . . .

E.W: That is the real paradox. If he were not mute, he would speak. It is only because he is mute . . . On the other hand, how can we transcend such a state?

September 8, 1981

NOTES

Introduction
1. Langer points out in *The Holocaust and the Literary Imagination* that the title of Borchert's essay intensifies the paradoxical quality of his work, since May represents Spring, the time of renewal, as well as the collapse of the Third Reich and the end of the war. Borchert returned to his homeland after the war, broken physically and spiritually, and died in 1947, at the age of 26.

Chapter 1
1. In "Elie Wiesel and Jewish Theology", Sherwin agrees with Steven S. Shwarzchild who called Wiesel "the high priest of our generation." Sherwin states: "Perhaps Wiesel is the rebbe. Perhaps he is our rebbe." In his essay, Sherwin

develops the notion that Wiesel's stories are his prayers. (Responses to Elie Wiesel)

2. T. W. Adorno was one of the first critics to express the view that it was not only impossible but immoral to write about the Holocaust. He was referring particularly to Paul Celan's poem "Todesfuge" which he found incongruously, and even "obscenely," lyrical. (Rosenfeld, "The Problematics of Holocaust Literature", 3)

3. Among the best-selling novels of the Holocaust are Gerald Green's *Holocaust*, Leslie Epstein's *King of the Jews* and William Styron's *Sophie's Choice*. Green's novel, based on the recent controversial television "docu-drama," attempts to encompass the totality of the Holocaust through various members of the Weiss family. As Barbara Foley states: "Green at once reduces agony to the status of melodrama and distorts the locus of historical responsibility"(355). *The King of the Jews*, while belonging to the irrealistic mode of fiction, leads to historical absurdism when applied to the fate of the city of Lodz. *Sophie's Choice*, a pseudo-factual novel, which has also received acclaim as a film of the Holocaust, misrepresents the event it claims to describe.

Chapter 2

1. Gad is not typical of "the messenger" in Wiesel's other novels, where he is usually presented as a stranger who brings the message from the dead to the living. In *Dawn* he is one of the leaders of the resistance movement in Palestine, and similarly, in *A Beggar in Jerusalem*, Gad is a Lieutenant Colonel in the Israeli army.

Chapter 3

1. Wiesel has used the Dialogue as a narrative form in two of is non-fiction works. In *A Jew Today* he presents three

"Dialogues": "A Father and His Son", "A Mother and Her Daughter" and "A Man and His Little Sister". The form of the dialogues suggests they took place in a concentration camp at the moment of separation between the speakers. In *One Generation After*, Wiesel devotes a chapter to "Dialogues 2" in which he presents eight short dialogues. This condensed mode of narrative is similar in many ways to a short poem.

Chapter 4
1. A parallel can be drawn between the first lines of *The Gates of the Forest* and the opening sentence of Melville's *Moby Dick*: "Call me Ishmael". Ishmael is a fictitious name of Biblical origin; no one in the novel calls the narrator Ishmael, only the reader is asked to do so. It is Ishmael, the only survivor of the Pequod catastrophe, who will retell the tale, echoing Job's words: "And I am escaped alone to tell thee".

Chapter 5
1. Rabbi Nahman's disciple, Nathan of Nemirov, preserved thirteen tales, published in 1815 under the title *Sippurey Ma'asiyot*. Most scholarship concerning Nahman's tales is focused on the original thirteen tales, which were originally printed in both Hebrew and Yiddish. Nahman himself designated these "accounts of deeds" as mythic tales.
2. In his commentary in *Beggars and Prayers*, Steinsaltz maintains that Nahman's final tale "The Seven Beggars", is "without doubt a magnificent conclusion to his work and a masterpiece from the point of view of both content and literary style"(171). It combines Biblical. Talmudic and Kabbalistic sources with worldly wisdom and elements of folk tales.
3. Ba'al Shem Tov, the Master of the Good Name, is the

founder of Hasidism and great grandfather of Rabbi Nachman.

4. The motif of spiritual quest is not common in the literature of Judaism. As Arthur Green points out in *Tormented Master*: "The idea that human life is a constant search for a hidden God would have struck most pre-modern Jewish authors as a rather strange one. God has already spoken, already revealed Himself and issued His command. The Jew, who has already stood at the foot of Sinai, does not usually see himself as a pilgrim".

Interview

1. Peretz Markish, born in 1895 in Soviet Russia, was a Yiddish poet, playwright and novelist, who expressed the modern trend in Yiddish and acclaimed the new Soviet revolution. His epic poem, "Brider", was among his best known published works. He was executed together with other Jewish writers in 1952.

WORKS BY WIESEL

Wiesel, Elie. *Night*. Trans. Stella Rodway. New York: Avon, 1960.
—*Dawn*. Trans. Frances Frenaye. London: Fontana, 1961.
—*The Accident*. Trans. Anne Borchardt. New York: Avon, 1962.
—*The Town Beyond the Wall*. Trans. Stephen Becker. New York: Avon, 1964.
—*The Gates of the Forest*. Trans. Frances Frenaye. New York: Avon, 1966.
—*The Jews of Silence*. Trans. Neal Kozody. New York: Holt, Rinehart and Winston, 1966.
—*Legends of Our Time*. New York: Holt, Rinehart and Winston, 1968.
—*A Beggar in Jerusalem*. Trans. Lily Edelman and the author. New York: Random House, 1970.
—*One Generation After*. Trans. Lily Edelman and the author. New York: Avon, 1970.
—*Souls on Fire*. Trans. Marion Wiesel. New York: Random House, 1972.
—*The Oath*. Trans. Marion Wiesel. New York: Random House, 1973.
—*Ani Maamin*. Trans. Marion Wiesel. New York: Random House, 1973.
—*Zalmen, or the Madness of God*. Trans. Nathan Edelman. New York: Random House, 1974.
—*Messengers of God*. Trans. Marion Wiesel. New York: Pocket Books, 1977.
—*A Jew Today*. Trans. Marion Wiesel. New York: Vintage, 1979.
—*Four Hasidic Masters*. Notre Dame: Univ. of Notre Dame Press, 1978.
—*The Trial of God*. Trans. Marion Wiesel. New York: Random House, 1979.
—*The Testament*. Trans. Marion Wiesel. New York: Summit, 1981.
—*Five Biblical Portraits*. Notre Dame: Univ. of Notre Dame Press, 1981.
—*Somewhere a Master*. Trans. Marion Wiesel. New York: Summit, 1982.
—*The Golem*. Trans. Anne Borchardt. Illus. Mark Podwal. New York: Summit, 1983.
—*The Fifth Son*. Trans. Marion Wiesel. New York: Summit, 1985.

BIBLIOGRAPHY

Abramowitz, Molly. *A Bibliography*. Metuchen, New Jersey: Scarecrow Press, 1974.

Alexander, Edward. *The Resonance of Dust*. Columbus: Ohio State Univ. Press, 1979.

Alter, Robert. *After the Tradition: Essays on Modern Jewish Writing*. New York: E.P. Dutton, 1969.

— "Between Hangman and Victim." *Responses to Elie Wiesel*. Ed. Harry James Cargas. New York: Persea, 1978.

Arnason, H. H. *A History of Modern Art*. London: Thames and Hudson, 1977.

Band, Arnold J. and Joseph Dan, eds. Nahman of Bratslav: The Tales. *The Classics of Western Spirituality*. New York: Paulist Press, 1978.

Berenbaum, Michael G. *The Vision of the Void: Theological Reflections on the Works of Elie Wiesel*. Middletown: Wesleyan Univ. Press, 1979.

— "Wiesel's Theory of the Holocaust." *Responses to Elie Wiesel*. Ed. Harry James Cargas. New York: Persea, 1978.

Berkovitz, Eliezer. *Faith After the Holocaust*. New York: Ktav Publishing House, 1973.

Booth, Wayne C. *The Rhetoric of Fiction*. Chicago: Univ. of Chicago Press, 1961.

Borchert, Wolfgang. "In May, in May Cried the Cuckoo." *The Man Outside*. Trans. David Porter. London: Calder and Boyars, 1966.

Brodhead, Richard A. *Hawthorne Melville and the Novel*. Chicago: Univ. of Chicago Press, 1947.

Brown, Robert McAfee. *Elie Wiesel: A Messenger to All Humanity*. Notre Dame: Univ. of Notre Dame Press, 1983.

Buber, Martin. *Jewish Mysticism and the Legends of Baalshem*. Trans. Lucy Cohen. London: J. M. Dent and Sons, 1931.

Burgess, Anthony. *The Novel Now*. London: Faber and Faber, 1971.

Camus, Albert. *The Myth of Sysyphus*. Trans. Justin O'Brien. Harmondsworth: Penguin, 1975.

Cargas, Harry James. *In Conversation with Elie Wiesel*. New York: Paulist Press, 1976.

—"Elie Wiesel: Christian Responses." *Responses to Elie Wiesel*. Ed. Harry James Cargas. New York: Persea, 1978.

Chatman, Seymour. *Story and Discourse in Fiction and Film*. Ithaca: Cornell Univ. Press, 1978.

Cohen, Arthur A. "Silence and Laughter." *Jewish Heritage* 84 Spring, 1966: 37-39.

Christ, Carol P. "Elie Wiesel's Stories: Still the Dialogue." *Dissertation Abstracts International* 35/07-A(Yale Univ, 1974)

Daiches, David. "After Such Knowledge . . ." *Commentary.* 40.6 (Dec. 1965): 105-110.

Des Pres, Terence. *The Survivor: An Anatomy of Life in the Death Camps.* New York: Oxford Univ. Press, 1976.

—"The Authority of Silence in Wiesel's Art." *Confronting the Holocaust.* Alvin Rosenfeld and Irving Greenberg, eds. Bloomington: Indiana Univ. Press, 1978.

Dostoyevsky, Fyodor. *The Brothers Karamazov.* Trans. David Magarshack. 2 vols. Harmondsworth: Penguin, 1958.

Edelman, Lily. "Opening the Hasidic Gates." *The National Jewish Monthly* (March, 1972): 72-77

Eliach, Yaffa. *Hasidic Tales of the Holocaust.* New York: Avon, 1983.

Estess, Ted. *Elie Wiesel.* New York: Ungar, 1980.

—"Elie Wiesel and the Drama of Interrogation." *Responses to Elie Wiesel.* Ed. Harry James Cargas. New York: Persea, 1 8.

Ezrahi, Sidra Dekoven. *By Words Alone.* Chicago: Univ. of Chicago Press, 1980.

Fackenheim, Emil L. *Encounters Between Judaism and Modern Philosophy.* New York: Schocken, 1980.

—*Quest for Past and Future.* Bloomington: Indiana Univ. Press, 1968.

—*The Jewish Return into History.* New York: Schocken, 1978.

Feldman, Irving. "After the Death Camps." *Commentary* 32(Dec. 1961): 262-264.

Fine, Ellen. *Legacy of Night.* Albany: State Univ. of New York Press, 1982.

"Dialogue with Elie Wiesel." *Centerpoint* 4(Fall, 1980): 19-25

"The Act of Listening." *Midstream* 27.7(Aug/Sep. 1981): 54-57

Foley, Barbara. "Fact, Fiction, Fascism: Testimony and Mimesis in Holocaust Narratives." *Comparative Literature* 34.4(Fall, 1982): 330-360

Friedlander, Albert H. Ed. *Out of the Whirlwind.* New York: Schocken, 1976.

Friedman, Maurice. *The Problematic Rebel.* Chicago: Univ. of Chicago Press, 1970.

— "The Job of Auschwitz." *Responses to Elie Wiesel.* Ed. Harry James Cargas. New York: Persea, 1978.

Garber, Frederick. "The Art of Elie Wiesel." *Judaism* 22(1973): 301-308.

Green, Arthur. *Tormented Master.* New York: Schocken, 1981.
Greenberg, Irving and Alvin Rosenfeld, eds. *Confronting the Holocaust.* Evanston: Northwestern Univ. Press, 1978.
Greenberg, Uri Zvi. "We were not likened to Dogs among Gentiles." *Modern Hebrew Poetry.* Ed. Ruth Finer. Berkeley: Univ. of California Press, 1968.
Halpern, Irving. *Messengers from the Dead.* Philadelphia: Westminster Press, 1970.
Indinopulos, Thomas A. "The Holocaust in the Stories of Elie Wiesel." *Responses to Elie Wiesel.* Ed. Harry James Cargas. New York: Persea, 1978.
Jacobson Roman. Ed. *Slavic Poetics.* The Hague: Mouton, 1973.
James, Henry. *The Art of the Novel.* New York: Charles Scribner's Son, 1962.
—"The New Novel." *Selected Literary Criticism.* Harmondsworth: Penguin, 1968.
Kafka, Frans. "In the Penal Settlement." *Metamorphosis and Other Stories.* Trans. Willa and Edwin Muir. Harmondsworth: Penguin, 1961.
Kaufmann, Walter. *The Faith of a Heretic.* New York: New American Library, 1978.
Keats, John. "Letters to George and Thomas Keats." *Selected Literary Criticism.* New York: Holt, Rinehart and Winston, 1969.
Knopp, Josephine. "Wiesel and the Absurd." *Contemporary Literature* 15(Winter, 1974): 213-220.
—"Elie Wiesel: Man, God and the Holocaust." *Midstream* (Aug/Sept. 1981): 45-57.
Langer, Lawrence. *The Age of Atrocity.* Boston: Beacon, 1978.
—*The Holocaust and the Literary Imagination.* New Haven: Yale Univ. Press, 1975.
—*Versions of Survival.* Albany: State Univ. of New York Press, 1982.
Leviant, Curt. "Elie Wiesel: A Soul on Fire." *SR: Books,* Jan, 1970.
Lifton, Robert Jay. *Death in Life: Survivors of Hiroshima.* New York: Harper and Row, 1965.
Malin, Irving. "Worlds Within Worlds." *Midstream* 20.2(Feb.1974): 79-82.
Mann, Thomas. *The Magic Mountain.* Harmondsworth: Penguin, 1960.
Mauriac, Francois. Forward. *Night.* New York: Avon, 1958.
McAfee Brown, Robert. *Messenger to All Humanity.* Notre Dame: Univ. of Notre Dame Press, 1983.
—"The Moral Society and the Work of Elie Wiesel." *Face to Face*

6(Spring, 1979): 22-27.

Melville, Herman. *Moby Dick*. New York: Signet, 1961.

Neher, Andre. *The Exile of the Word*. Trans. David Maisel. Philadelphia: The Jewish Publication Society of America, 1981.

The New York Times Magazine. (Oct. 23, 1983): 32-69. Samuel G. Freedman. "Bearing Witness: The Life and Work of Elie Wiesel."

Olson, Alan M. Ed. *Myth Symbol and Reality*. Notre Dame: Univ. of Notre Dame Press, 1980.

Pawel, Ernst. "Fiction of the Holocaust." *Midstream* (June/July, 1970): 14-26

Pickard, Max. *The World of Silence*. South Bend, Indiana: Regnery/Gateway, 1952.

Raban, Jonathan. *The Technique of Modern Fiction*. London: Edward Arnold, 1968.

Robert, Marthe. *Frans Kafka's Loneliness*. Trans. Ralph Manhem. London: Faber and Faber, 1982.

Romberg, Bertil. *Studies in the Narrative Technique of the First-Person Novel*. Stolkholm: Almquist and Wiksell, 1962.

Rosenberg, Harold. *The Tradition of the New*. London: Paladin, 1970.

Rosenfeld, Alvin H. A Double Dying: *Reflections on Holocaust Literature*. Bloomington: Indiana Univ. Press, 1980

—"The Problematics of Holocaust Literature." *Confronting the Holocaust: The Impact of Elie Wiesel*. Alvin Rosenfeld, and Irvin Greenberg, eds. Bloomington: Indiana Univ. Press, 1978.

"The Need to Transmit." *Midstream* 28 (Jan. 1982): 51-53.

Roskies, David G. *Against the Apocalypse*. Cambridge: Harvard Univ. Press, 1984.

Roth, John K. *A Consuming Fire:* Encounters with Elie Wiesel. Atlanta: John Knox Press, 1979.

Rousset, David. *The Other Kingdom*. Trans. Roman Guthrie. New York: Reynal and Hitchcock, 1947.

Sartre, Jean-Paul. *What is Literature?* Trans. Bernard Frechtman. New York: Reynal and Hitchcock, 1947.

Schapiro, Meyer. "Style." *Aesthetics Today*. Morris Philipson and Paul J. Gudel, eds. New York: New American Library, 1980.

Scholem, Gershom G. *Major Trends in Jewish Mysticism*. New York: Schocken, 1961.

Sherwin, Byron. "Elie Wiesel and Jewish Theology." *Responses to Elie Wiesel*. Ed. Harry James Cargas. New York: Persea, 1978.

"Elie Wiesel on Madness." *CCAR Journal* 19(June 1972): 25-32.

Skloot, Robert. Ed. *The Theatre of the Holocaust*. Wisconsin: Univ of Wisconsin Press, 1982.
Smith, Lacey Baldwin. Ed. *Dimensions of the Holocaust*. Evanston: Northwestern Univ. 1977.
Solzhenitsyn, Alexander. *One Day in the Life of Ivan Denisovich*. Trans. Ralph Parker. Harmondsworth: Penguin, 1963.
Stanzel, Frans. *Narrative Situations in the Novel*. Trans. James P. Pusack.Bloomington: Indiana Univ. Press, 1971.
— "Second Thoughts on *Narrative Situations in the Novel*." Novel 2(Spring, 1978): 247-262.
Steiner, George. *After Babel*. London: Oxford Univ. Press, 1975.
— *Language and Silence*. Harmondsworth: Penguin, 1979.
Steinsaltz, Adin. *Beggars and Prayers*. New York: Basic Books, 1979.
Sternberg, Meir. *Expositional Modes and Temporal Ordering in Fiction*. Baltimore: John Hopkins Univ. Press, 1978.
Talmon, J. L. "European History as the Seedbed of the Holocaust." *Holocaust and Rebirth*. Jerusalem: R. H. Hacohen Press, 1974.
Uspensky, Boris. A Poetics of Composition. Trans. Valentina Zavarin and Susan Wittig. Berkeley: Univ. of California Press, 1973.
Visser, N.W. "The Novelistic Documentary." Doct. Dissertation, Rhodes Univ. 1972.
—"The Generic Identity of the Novel." *Novel*. 10-11(Winter, 1978): 101-114.
— "An Aspectual Approach to the Novel." *Communique* 5.2(1980): 475-54.
— "Temporal Vantage Point in the Novel." The Journal of *Narrative Technique*. 7.2(Spring, 1977): 81-93.
Weiss-Rosmarin, Trude. "Hasidism – Authentic and Inauthentic." *Jewish Spectator* 37(1972): 6-9.
Wieseltier, Leon. "History as Myth." *Commentary* 57.1(Jan. 1974): 66-70.
Wiesel, Elie. "The Holocaust as Literary Inspiration." *Dimensions of the Holocaust*. Evanston: Northwestern University, 1977.
Young, James. "Believing in Holocaust Literature." *Midstream* (April, 1983): 60-61.

ABOUT THE AUTHOR

Mona Berman – (B.A., Wits; B.A. Hons., R.A.U.; B.Ed., Wits; M.A.Rhodes University) was born and lives in Johannesburg, is a mother of four daughters and a grandmother to many grandchildren. She has worked as a freelance journalist and has published several articles on Holocaust literature. She promotes, sells and curates exhibitions of talented young South African visual artists. She has recently published her first novel.

The author wishes to thank SAJACT (The South African Jewish Art and Culture Trust) for their support.